The Other Side of the Badge

Badge

by Russell Ford, Ph.D.

Disclaimer

This book is dedicated to all my brothers and sisters who wear the badge, placing their lives on the line every day to protect others. I also dedicate this book to my parents, who encouraged me to follow my dream of being in law enforcement despite their having to worry every day when I went to work. To my kids, who had to deal with changing plans and broken promises because of work schedules and court subpoenas. Finally, to my wife, who stood by my side throughout most of my career and still does to this day, who had to deal with my ups and downs, wondering if I would make home at the end of the day: I love you more than life itself.

Table of Contents

Part I: Introduction

"Bravery is not the absence of fear but action in the face of fear."

—Unknown

Throughout my career, I have been to numerous seminars, training sessions, and team-building events about the psychological trauma officers face in their jobs every day. However, this was not something talked about when I started my career in the early 1990s. No mention was ever made of what officers can go through in their careers and the long-term damage the trauma can cause, both professionally and personally. Not all officers will face psychological issues during their careers. There are some who will never have to face a homicide, suicide, major car accident, or any other type of incident considered to be critical. There are some who will never pull their weapon in the line of duty. There is still an abundance of officers who will face those incidents time and again. Back when I started, the "old school" way of thinking became an issue. *"We are tough and should be able to handle anything. Nobody should ever see us get upset." "Cops don't cry or whine. They just move on."* You get the idea.

Several years and many incidents later, around the mid-2000s, departments really started to look at the trauma officers face over the long-term of doing the job. Officers thought nobody wanted to listen to them. The prevalent attitude could be described in this way: Bury your issues, put the bad stuff in that little box in the back of your mind, man up, and move forward.

By that time, I was considered one of the "old school" guys, only because that is who I'd learned from and the mentality I'd acquired. Some thought I had been a cop for a lot longer than I had been. I just kept moving forward, going from one call to the next, never stopping to think about that dead body, the child who had died, or the victim who had been sexually assaulted. I learned that nobody wanted to hear about the horrendous calls for service during the day or how I felt about them.

I would have negative thoughts that discouraged me from seeking help: *"Just stop whining. You signed up for this job. They didn't sign you up."* One friend had been murdered in the line of duty, and three had taken their own lives. The homicide was bad enough, but losing three more to suicide was making my mindset worse.

I never turned to alcohol or drugs to deal with my issues, as many might. Again, I would just put those issues in the back of my mind in a little box and hope they would go away. However, the dark memories would resurface later in thoughts and dreams. I have seen many police officers turn to alcohol or drugs to ease the pain. Those were not my vices. My only crutch was tobacco, which was bad enough. I also had anger issues, along with a mistrust of those I didn't know—and even of some I did know.

I started distancing myself from those who were close to me, as that seemed to be the best thing. I can't truly say death hadn't crossed my mind; I wasn't brave enough to take my own life but, at times, I thought it would be easier. I'm not sure where it came from or when it started. Sure, I had money issues at times, relationship problems early on, nightmares every so often, and just flat-out didn't want to be around people on my days off. I believe I never went that far because I had lost a couple of friends to suicide and had seen the damage it did to their families. It only brought pain to everyone, leaving the loved ones left behind with the question, "Why did no one see it coming?"

Sometimes, it takes just one training and the right person to make you realize what is happening to you psychologically, physically, and mentally. I know many don't want to hear it, but there are people out there who are willing to listen. I was one who didn't want to talk; nor did I believe there was anybody out there who could help me. I figured, "They haven't done the job, so how can they tell me how to fix myself? They haven't seen what I have or dealt with what I have."

It was easy to walk away from friends because I refused to let myself get close to anybody. I thought keeping my distance would make it hurt less if someone else decided to take their own life, and make it hurt others less if something happened to me. The whole purpose of this book is to let all first responders know they are not alone; it is also for those who may not understand what is going on with their loved ones or friends. Those who are not in some type of first-responder position will watch their family member, significant other, parent, or friend change and may not understand why, what is happening, or how to "fix it."

When I decided to work toward my PhD in Forensic Psychology, I wanted to understand the psychological effects officers endured during their careers and how to deal with such trauma beyond turning to chemical abuse or suicide. I understood I had changed from the time I started my career, and I wanted to learn why such things had impacted me so hard and how to find my way back from the mental trauma we all go through. I spent years helping those who could not help themselves. Now, I want to help those who have been placed in the same situations I went through.

I also wanted to understand why criminals commit the crimes they do and how some can cause so much pain and suffering without their conscience taking over. The criminal mind is intriguing and interesting, and I wanted to learn more about it.

I know some who are reading this will probably say the psychological issues are bullshit. They have never had feelings of distress or anxiety during their time on the job. At the same time, they feel the need to be tough. However, it's the things that eat at us over time—the reoccurring visions, nightmares, or reminders—that break us down. I have heard time and again from psychologists who came to the department about the importance of getting the right help. They placed great emphasis on self-care and not allowing things to get to one's head. All in all, they told us not to take the job personally.

One psychologist stated, "If you don't take it personally, it won't bother you as much." That's some good advice coming from someone who has never dealt with death at a homicide scene, the continued abuse taken from the public, or just the everyday calls consisting of violence. How can officers not take certain calls personally—whether it's someone calling you names and just trying to piss you off, or dealing with a child victim of a crime who's the same age as a child close to you, or seeing a person you've been trying to help for a long time become a murder victim? How could *anyone* not take these issues personally?

To me, not having an emotional response to certain calls is a sign of being a psychopath. No matter how hard we may try to hide our feelings, they come out eventually, one way or another. It may happen later, when the officer is alone in their patrol car, on the way home, or even after they reach home several days later. It's not even about taking things personally. We are just human, and we aren't emotionless.

Even changes made within the department can affect an officer. Officers learn to live up to the expectations of their department, and when more restrictions or harsher penalties are imposed, it's a hard hit to those officers. They may feel the changes are a direct attack on them. When no explanation is provided, it makes them wonder who fucked shit up enough for such strict changes to be necessary, and this suspicion can be taken personally.

It pisses people off when one screwball makes a mistake and everyone in the department has to pay the penalty. That's like spanking all your children when a single child gets into trouble. Often when a department makes stricter policies for everyone because one officer decided to do something stupid, it is assumed more officers will make the same mistake. Sometimes, these policies are written just in case that does happen, causing the rest of the department to feel distrusted by those in power.

It is easy to tell others what to look for as far as challenges one may go through, how to deal with difficult calls, and how to handle changes made in a department. However, it is not easy to get others to understand and deal with those changes or emotions they may have difficulty getting rid of. It is even harder to talk to those who think it will never happen to them and then later wonder how they got into such a dark place in their life. However, when an individual has seen numerous homicides—and I responded to only a couple or so at my last department—numerous suicides, child abuse in its many different stages (up to and including death), and juvenile overdoses, they are bound to get a little messed up in the head.

Again, there will be some who say this is all bullshit—but they could be the same ones who continue to have nightmares or need several cocktails to sleep at night. There are some who are still not willing to get the help they need, despite having children, being divorced, and dealing with custody cases or troubles at home. According to these officers and first responders, their problems are not caused by them, but by everyone else: their spouse doesn't like their job because it takes up too much time, the kids are always in trouble, and people just want more and more. They refuse to consider the possibility that the issue may be them, not those around them.

What is not realized by many is the toxic environment we may create outside the job. We end up being hypervigilant all the time, both on and off duty, which can be a cause for burnout. We start hanging out with those who think like us—meaning we only hang out with other cops—and complain about the negatives, whether from calls or from inside the department. Burnout is a very serious issue; we lose touch with doing the things we like, or we give up on getting to know people outside the job. This is not a healthy environment for anybody. It causes us to think about the job all the time, keeping us in a dangerous mindset.

Each year, more than 150 police officers commit suicide within the United States alone. This kind of tragic outcome isn't limited just to police officers, either. It is an issue with all first responders. More than 100 US firefighters take their own lives each year, as well, and paramedics and nurses also suffer psychological trauma. PTSD is a real thing among first responders; many people think the term is thrown around too flippantly, or used by some as an excuse, but it absolutely is real.

At one time, it was believed that only those who had been to war and engaged in combat suffered from PTSD— or shellshock, as it once was known. However, we are finding out this is not the case. First responders may not be on the battlefield every day, but there is a war taking place in their own neighborhoods and familiar streets. They still see plenty of trauma and respond to plenty of critical incidents during their career, some sooner than others.

When I realized on my own what was happening to me, I knew I needed to do something about it. I never received professional help, which has been a regret later in my life. My help was learning more about what was happening to me and recognizing how much I had changed in such a short period of time. That realization was a cause for me to continue furthering my education, which is exactly what I did.

I now have a PhD in Forensic Psychology. Doing the work to obtain this degree allowed me to learn about police psychology and the psychological trauma connected to the job. Don't ever think it is something that just goes away. It has to be worked on every day, in every part of your life. I have been retired for several years and still work every day not letting my past trauma affect me. I also teach criminal justice classes at two colleges in hopes to help others understand what they are getting into when they enter the criminal justice system. Wanting to help others understand what I am about to tell you on how my career got started—and how it ended. I'm going to reveal the difficulties I faced during the in-between and the after. I hope it will hit home, and that reading these words will help you know there is help and hope for you.

Part II: Chasing the Dream

"In this family, no one fights alone."

—Unknown

The Academy

When I was a child, I would watch all the cop shows—*Hill Street Blues, Hawaii Five-0, T.J. Hooker.* I always thought they were so cool, busting the bad guys, getting into shootouts, putting the criminals away, and then back to work they'd go. "Book 'em, Dano" was the line that always stuck in my head. I always wanted to say that one line during a stakeout with a partner in a two-man car, ready to "kick some ass." I also looked up to the sheriffs from tales of the Old West—Pat Garrett and Wyatt Earp, the well-known lawmen of the west. I grew up getting to know a couple of local officers in the town where I lived. I respected how they acted and how they dealt with us kids. They were definitely guys to model after.

I knew I wanted to be an officer of the law when I grew up, so I didn't have college on my mind. I was an average student and knew I didn't need a college degree to be a police officer, like the sheriffs I saw in movies and on TV. When I turned 18, I knew that any trouble I got into would stay on my adult record, so I did my best to stay out of it—or at least avoid getting caught. Driving was my biggest issue. I loved driving fast whenever I had the opportunity. Of course, that came with its penalties, as well.

When I was twenty-two and living in a different city, I found a police academy close to where I lived. It took me a year to save for the academy, and once I had the money, I signed up. It's not always the case that you get hired by a police department that will send you to their academy and pay you for it. However, if you are willing to pay for it yourself, there are ways to get in—usually through a community college, which is what I did. So, I joined my first police academy: twenty-six weeks of attending night classes while working full-time during the day. It wasn't cheap, but it was cheaper than getting a degree, and it was a hell of a lot more fun. The lead academy instructors were two retired officers out of Los Angeles. They were kind of salty and liked to yell, but they were also professional and friendly.

Of course, they would bring in other instructors to teach us about the laws, driving, shooting, arrest tactics, and so on. These instructors had experience in police work and would tell stories of the good times they had when they were beat cops, driving around in their cars and going after the bad guys. They also shared the experiences they'd had in courtrooms so we would know how to act. I remember thinking back then, "This is definitely for me. It's just like in the shows I used to watch as a kid."

The instructors made it look glorious and sound like a bunch of fun. So, I continued in the academy, knowing I would be out one day doing the same things they talked about doing. Some classes were boring, like constitutional law and learning the state statutes. Yet many were interesting, too: arrest control, the firing range, pepper spray protocol, and the driving courses (which were my favorites). They were fun and exciting classes that really got my adrenaline pumping. They made every bit of the job look so appealing.

I mean, where else can you use arrest control moves that hurt like hell on people, get into physical altercations, and get paid for it? Even firefighters don't have that much fun! Cops would get to kick in doors and search through people's personal stuff all because a judge said there was enough probable cause to do so. If the person didn't comply with what they were told, the officers would get to slam them on the ground and throw handcuffs on them with the sole purpose of taking them to jail.

People who broke driving laws would get pulled over. Being in a hurry was not a valid excuse. We learned we could hold drivers for up to twenty minutes while conducting a traffic stop if they had an attitude. So many things could be done to people who disrespected you or pissed you off—if you wore a badge.

For six months, my daily routine consisted of working my day job, heading to school for a quick workout before class, listening to lectures during class, learning about tactics, laws, and ethics, and then going home and starting again. Some nights meant staying up late to study for a quiz or test the next day or to complete a written assignment; it could include anything from talking about constitutional rights or state laws to writing a report based on a scenario provided during class.

In driving class, we were continuously told to go faster while moving around one-foot-tall traffic cones; the goal was not to hit the children (cones). We would drive forward and then have to drive in reverse. Every time a cone was hit, someone would yell "CRASH!" and claim I'd just hit their kids. Being yelled at was a reason to work hard. At the end of the academy, we knew how to stay alert at all times, keep both hands on the wheel, and drive fast without wrecking the car. It never really crossed my mind that, at some point in my career, it would become the norm to be driving with one hand at high speeds, operating a radio, looking at a map, reading dispatch notes, and eating at the same time.

Firearms days involved a lot of shooting at things that did not move; silhouettes were the common target. Beyond that, we also learned about moving tactics, clearing buildings, shooting from cars, and using a blasting chord to blow open doors—a little added bonus. Officers always had to make sure they didn't shoot the innocent people pictured on the targets. We had to make sure our shots were effective and accurate. This was not a time to get our feelings hurt because we got yelled at. At some point, one of our instructors would shout, "What the fuck did you just do? You just took out Granny Good Nickle, and now you and your department are being sued!"

On simunition day, we used paint-filled, low-energy, live rounds. We learned shot placement really fast during this time. Running through real-life scenarios using these live rounds helped with making sure our shots counted. Otherwise, we would be shot by the suspect or an instructor or shoot one of the observers considered innocent bystanders. We also learned really fast that getting hit with a simunition paint round was painful.

If we did not have enough padding, the paint rounds would leave welts the size of dinner plates wherever they would hit. This was a lesson learned the first time we ran these scenarios, and nobody believed the instructors when they said to wear a lot of padded clothing. I, unfortunately, was shot several times on our first day. My back and chest were very colorful in the days that followed.

The first scenario we ran through was an individual sitting on a set of stairs leading to what appeared to be the front door of a residence. As I came around the corner of the building, I made contact with the party and started talking to him as if we were there to investigate a possible crime. My cover officer was standing to the side of me, on my left and slightly back a little, as we were to be watching out for any potential threats that may be present.

The problem was that my cover was focused on the person sitting on the stairs, as well, so neither of us saw the other guy come from around the corner of a building behind us. My partner took the first several hits with the rounds. By the time I saw him react out of the corner of my eye, it was too late. As I pulled my weapon and turned around, I was struck in the back of my leg, on my back, and in the chest; I had no chance. After a good lecture from the instructors about making sure to keep a 360-degree watch at all times, we moved on to the next scenario, which was a simulated traffic stop.

Again, I was the contact officer approaching the driver's side of the vehicle. My cover was approaching the passenger side. As I was approaching the driver, I noticed him moving his arm around to the front of him. As I was pulling my weapon, the driver brought up a weapon, as well, and began firing at me. I was firing back in return while falling backward onto the ground and trying to move away.

I only got hit with one round from this scenario, but it was in the left shoulder and hurt like hell. I never hit the driver, but I did break the side mirror with one of my rounds. The vehicle belonged to one of the instructors, and he was not happy. After getting yelled at for breaking the side mirror, my response was to talk back and tell him he shouldn't have brought his own vehicle if he planned on having someone shoot at me. I basically told him it was his fault. My punishment? I had to run two miles while the rest of the class went through their scenarios. But I didn't get shot again that day.

Overall, it was a blast; and in the end, it was going to make my career even better—plus, at least I would know how to pay attention and not just wait to get shot. Learning arrest control tactics were just as painful, in a different way, as being shot with a simunition. The twisting and turning of arms and bodies left one sore for several days. But again, it would all be worth it when the academy was over because we would know how to use the control techniques on people who just wouldn't want to listen.

During the six-month academy, you made contacts with other police officers, forming friendships that last a long time. Most who were in the academy with me were like-minded people and had the same goals. Some had the desire to work in small towns. Others wanted to work in the big city where the crimes were numerous, dealing with murders and robberies. They wanted to be where the likelihood of getting into fights on the job was great and the criminals were plentiful. We would build a community within the academy, working out together, studying, practicing arrest control, and even hanging out on the weekends. Even after the academy, we would get together and celebrate when someone would get a job, marking each other's successes, accomplishments, and fulfillments of post-academy dreams. At that time, those wanting to become police officers planned for it to be a career. They had no intention of just doing the job for a paycheck. Back then, people weren't cops for the pay. They did the job because it was a dream, a career, a way to help those who could not help themselves. The academy was paramilitary; every workout and action taken was taught by veterans, and this was the way we were trained to be police officers. Discipline, integrity, honor, and ethics were pounded into our heads for so many weeks.

Unfortunately, joining an academy through a community college meant almost anyone was allowed in as long as they were paying. One of our classmates had a warrant for his arrest at the start of the academy, but none of us knew about it until five weeks in. In the middle of class, two local officers came into the classroom. We were learning about constitutional law at the time. They took this classmate into custody and walked him out in handcuffs and across the campus to their patrol vehicles. There was no concern with shame or trying to hide someone being arrested. We never saw him again, though. I'm not sure whether that was due to his embarrassment or his being kicked out of the class. On the day we had to go to the shooting range, we noticed we were missing another classmate. He had been present for the classroom portion of firearms class and learning how to clean and operate a weapon but was not present for the actual range day. We later came to find out that he was a convicted felon and could not be around firearms. It's amazing what you learn about people in academies like these. Neither would have ever been hired into a police department, but they were paying to go through an academy.

When the time came to look for a job, we were all guilty of providing the textbook answer of why we wanted to become police officers: "To help others." Of course, the real reason was never talked about when applying for a job; departments will not hire someone who gives the answer, "To kick ass and arrest the bad guy!" This answer would not be revealed until later in life. Some in the academy would never get a job because of their history prior to the academy—drug use or arrests—but most would. Most started in small departments, later moving to larger agencies.

The one thing that was noticed many years later was the impact the career would have on our mental and physical health, along with the strain it would place on our family life and friends. We were not told about these costs of becoming police officers.

Part III: Wearing the Badge

"Police officers put the badge on every morning, not knowing for sure if they'll come home at night to take it off."

—Tom Cotton

Putting On the Badge

After the academy, I received my first job with a small sheriff's department in a decent-sized county. Within this county were a few mountain towns; three had their own departments but were also small. My first job was as an animal control officer and deputy when coverage or backup was needed. After I was sworn in by the Sheriff and received my badge, I was told to return for duty on Monday morning. I was so excited to begin my new career of "enforcing laws and kicking ass."

I was so excited I really couldn't sleep the night before. I was anxious to get up and afraid to miss the alarm. Ready to start, I put on that uniform, strapped on the first pistol I have ever owned, a Ruger 357 Security Six, and was ready to go. When the time came, I was out the door. I showed up for work half an hour early to receive my identification card, meet all my coworkers, and fill out the documents needed for emergency contact information and taxes.

Upon arrival, I was let into the front door and told to sit in the patrol room and wait for someone from Human Resources to come and get me. Others were already there, typing reports and talking. I was approached by one of the older deputies, who introduced himself as Gary and told me he had been in the department for twenty-something years. Gary shared that he had been a truck driver for several years before getting hired on to the sheriff's department. Our conversation helped me relax a little, and we started talking about the trucking career because my dad was also working as a truck driver at the time. Gary got tired of being gone all the time and wanted a change, something that would get him home every night to spend time with his family.

During this conversation, Gary stopped abruptly and told me there was something he needed to make sure I understood very clearly. Intrigued, I said, "Okay. What is that?" He told me that every new cop has an issue with being badge-heavy, and that is not something he wanted to see from me. It was the quickest way out of the job and a hard lesson to learn sometimes. The badge on my shirt was no heavier than the few ounces it weighed.

He told me he knew being a cop for the first time made me feel like I was powerful, and that the badge would help me feel like Superman. But I needed to remember that I was brand new on the job and knew nothing as far as he was concerned. I was green. I was wet behind the ears. He told me if he ever saw me acting like an asshole, trying to be tough or cool, expecting people to do what I said just because I thought I could, it would be a mistake.

Gary said if he ever saw me act like that, he was going to take matters into his own hands and kick my ass himself. He told me I had to earn that right and had to learn early not to be an asshole, or he would make sure I would be taken down a notch or two as soon as he noticed or heard about it. For some reason, I believed Gary; this was kind of a blow to my ego on the very first day, straight out of the gate. Here I was, young and dumb, ready to kick some ass, and I was being knocked down right away.

This was definitely something I did not expect to hear on my first day. I wasn't sure what to think; should I laugh, or should I be afraid? What I did know was that Gary was the one I wanted to learn from. He was straight to the point and no bullshit. I wanted to be just like Gary—a no-bullshit guy. Shortly after, the other deputies introduced themselves. They all informed me Gary was serious and that I'd better watch how I wore the badge.

The only honorable way to wear that badge was to follow orders, listen to what others told me, and treat everybody with respect no matter who they were. This put some fear into me. I wanted to make sure to live up to the standards of those around me, those I worked with. I wanted to learn from the older guys in the department; they obviously had the techniques necessary to be successful and respected.

Once the required documents were completed, I started my training in animal control. I was taught how to fill out the forms, take care of the animals in the shelter, and read the county map. I was trained in referencing complaints, making contact with citizens, and licensing their pets. I was introduced to all the veterinarians in the county, as well as the wolf-hybrid owners. I was also taught how to properly handle a wolf-hybrid in case I had to pick one up. These dogs were commonly owned in this county, and many people had no real idea how to handle them or keep them penned properly.

The first two weeks on the job were nothing but learning my role and showing I retained what I was taught. After two weeks of training, I set out on my own to enforce the animal control laws. During the next month, when I had downtime, I was trained here and there on the road as a deputy so I would know all aspects of the job. I was taught how to write reports, file cases, write traffic tickets, investigate crimes, and secure a crime scene if I was the first to respond. On several occasions, I would arrive as a backup officer since I was in the area. I had the ability to cover shifts when the patrol was low on manpower, cover deputies during calls, and respond to calls as needed if something good was going down.

My daily duties consisted primarily of taking animal calls and performing follow-up on animal control issues, such as barking dog complaints, dogs at large, and animal neglect and abuse. I would also collect animal license receipts and payments as necessary while contacting a citizen for that purpose. I would pick up stray dogs and take them back to the shelter until their owners were found or until they were adopted out, check on reports of malnourished cattle and horses, and work closely with animal rescue organizations.

I have to say I truly enjoyed this work. It taught me a lot about how these organizations operate and how hard they work to find homes for all dogs. There was always hope for a no-kill shelter; however, there did come a time when I had to euthanize my first dog due to the age and illness of the dog. There were dogs unable to be adopted; nobody wanted to take on an elderly dog with large expenses and such a short time of life remaining, or the dog that was so mean no person could get close to it—that would've been a very difficult task, emotionally. I was hoping to go through my time not having to euthanize any dogs, but I always knew there was a chance I would have to.

Hard Choices

I had received a five-minute training on which medications to use, the order in which to use them, and how much to administer a few months previously. My supervisor was on vacation for this first one, so I took the medications out of the cabinet and grabbed a needle.

The dog I had to put down was a small white elderly poodle someone had left at a vacant house. Since they were renters, I was unable to locate them, and there was no forwarding address given to the actual homeowner. This was one of those cases in which I would have enjoyed finding these people and giving them a ticket for animal cruelty. I guessed how much of each drug to give the poodle and walked back to where the dogs were kenneled. This was the first of many hard days to come, as I hated having to put down an animal.

I held the dog in my lap and gave him the first of the medications; it was an anesthesia to place him into a hard sleep, like an anesthetic for surgery. Once he was asleep, I had to inject the main drug, called Pentobarbital, directly into his heart. It kind of looked like Pepto-Bismol. With tears in my eyes, I sat in the kennel with this old guy, just the two of us in the building, and injected the final drug. He passed on very peacefully while I sat on the floor holding him and crying a little. Yes, I will admit it: I did cry when I had to complete this terrible task. Once it was done, I took his body to a nearby vet to have him cremated. I was thankful it was on my Friday. The next three days consisted of camping and fishing, which was what I enjoyed doing—having the ability to not have to think about work and relax.

During my time in this position, I had to put down a total of three dogs, which was not bad for the number of dogs we would have in and out of the shelter throughout my time in the department. The last dog was like the first, just elderly and dropped at the shelter because the owners no longer wanted the hindrance of having to deal with an old and sick dog. The second dog was not old.

It was a black chow and meaner than the Devil himself. We could not let him out of the kennel and had to use a pole with a loop on the end to hold him back while we cleaned out his crate. He would try to attack us every time we put food and water into his kennel. We came across him during a traffic accident. His owner had a heart attack while driving and was taken to the hospital by ambulance.

The medics were having a difficult time trying to get to the owner because the dog was snarling and snapping at them. At the time, we figured it was because the dog was scared. After some time, we realized the dog was just mean. After a couple of weeks of holding on to this dog, we were told the owner had passed away and had no other family members to take the dog. Since there was no way we would be able to adopt this dog out, the only other option was to put him down. It was still not an easy task. I didn't like the idea of putting a dog down any more than I had the first time, but it had to be done.

Since we couldn't get close to this dog, the only way we could give the anesthesia was to take the pole with the loop on the end, hook it around his neck like a leash, and pull him toward us against the kennel door. I truly did not like this idea, but it was really the only option we had. Thankfully, I had a partner working with me, as this was a two-man job. After finally injecting enough anesthesia to put down an elephant, the dog went to sleep, and the rest was easier to complete.

I was thankful for the rescue groups we had in the county. Without them, we probably would have had to put down more dogs, since we didn't have the time or manpower to attend adoption functions. We would hang on to a dog for ten days after we picked it up or it was brought in. This was to help watch for any illnesses and to see if the owner would show and claim their pet. After ten days, we would reach out to one of the five rescue groups within the county, and they would come and take the dog off our hands to find it a good home. Before I started working at this agency, there were at least two dogs put down a month, and I wanted to change that way of thinking.

License, Please

Every Monday morning was the start of a new week and a new adventure. So many things could happen. I never knew where my day would take me. After so many years, it's hard to say which time during my employment certain things happened. When I was with the sheriff's department, I contacted many people about getting their dogs licensed within the county and let them know they would receive a ticket if they did not comply. Of course, I would get yelled at by pet owners, given the excuse that it costs too much, or end up dealing with those who just didn't acknowledge the warning. I also met a lot of people who were thankful for the reminder.

Every once in a while, you come across one person who makes the job memorable. There was one in particular who will always stick in my mind. I had responded to a secluded house in a subdivision placed back in the woods and surrounded by thick trees. The neighbors could not see each other; they were separated by several acres on each lot, which made it completely private.

I knocked on the door of this house. I got no response, but dogs could be heard barking inside the house, so I knocked again. Assuming nobody was home, I placed a business card and license renewal card in the hinge of the front door and started walking away. As I got close to my patrol car, I heard a female voice behind me ask if she could help me. I turned around to tell her the reason for my visit— it was just a reminder about her dog license renewal.

I was stopped mid-sentence by the attire she was wearing. This was a forty-something-year-old female wearing a bathrobe that was not tied in the front. She was standing outside, and in front of me, wearing absolutely nothing under a wide-open green bathrobe. I have no idea why she was even wearing the robe at all, since she didn't close it.

Now, being in my early twenties and having never considered this would happen, not even through the stories I had heard from the other deputies about dealing with naked people, one could imagine how much it took me by surprise. She was in pretty good shape for her age—or so I thought at the time. She was not afraid to show herself off to a perfect stranger.

I was working hard at keeping my composure and keeping my eyes on her face while talking to her about her dog licenses being renewed. This was difficult. She continued walking toward me and stopped about four or five feet in front of me—you know, that safe distance we try to keep between us and other people. I was explaining the penalties if she didn't comply, and she stood there and smiled. I told her if she didn't have the license purchased within one week, I would return and have to issue a ticket for her to appear in court for failure to comply with dog licensing laws. She began smiling even more and asked if that was a promise, and I told her it was. She told me she was tempted to let it happen and, next time, maybe she'd be wearing absolutely nothing.

Maintaining professionalism as best I could, I told her I didn't want to write that ticket and that she should make sure to get those licenses purchased. In the back of my mind, however, I was wondering, or maybe even hoping, I would have to go back—just to see what would really happen. She said she understood and walked back into her house. Of course, there is a reason the more experienced officers don't tell the newbies about these kinds of situations; it's more fun to watch them fumble through on their own. My telling the other deputies about what had happened only made them laugh. They remembered their first times dealing with such situations and shared their stories.

Over the next week, I was watching to make sure she got her licenses for her dogs; on the day I was to respond to write that ticket, I did receive notification she had complied. I was still kind of hoping she would make me return. But she had heard my warning and taken care of what she was supposed to, after all.

Throughout that year, I would go on many more animal control calls and take in more dogs, including a wolf-hybrid I had taken in three times for running at large. One morning, I walked into the shelter and opened the door where the dogs lived. As I did, I noticed this animal walking in the middle aisle between all the caged dogs. It took my breath away for a minute. She was very large, and it was the last thing I expected to walk into. The top of her head came to the bottom of my ribs, and I'm not a short man.

I looked at her, and she looked back at me. I thought, "Well shit. This could be interesting, getting her back into the kennel." I immediately closed the door to keep her contained and remembered what I was taught by several owners of these animals in the area who knew how to raise and keep these dogs safe. I was told, unless I was ready for a fight, to never look them directly in the eyes. This action was confrontational to a wolf-hybrid; it can be for any dog, but these animals would seriously take it as a challenge. I was also told to never stand over the top of them. It could make them feel they were being cornered and would cause them to attack.

So, without hesitation, I took my duty belt off, placed it on my desk, took a deep breath, and walked into the kennel area where she was running. I didn't want anything on my belt to cause her to spook. As I walked in, I took another deep breath and closed the door behind me, got down on one knee to her level, looked her right in the eyes, and asked her, "What the fuck you gonna do now?" Of course, I was concerned this may not have been the smartest move, keeping one hand on the handle of the door in case I needed a quick escape.

At first, she started to snarl at me, and I really thought, "Oh shit, this may have been a mistake. Nothing like putting chum in the water to attract a shark." We sat there and stared at each other for what seemed like forever. In fact, it was just a couple of minutes. All at once, she started wagging her tail, walked over to me, laid down, and put her head in my lap. The next thing I knew, I was petting this big and "dangerous" wolf-hybrid like she was a tamed mutt. This was the day I realized that wolf- hybrids aren't as scary and mean as I'd been led to believe.

After I got her outside in a large dog pen and played some fetch with her, I put her back into the kennel and rigged a top on her crate so she couldn't escape again. Any time she was found running after that, she would come right over to me. Hell, she wouldn't even do that with her owners.

Sometimes, you just have to take the bull by the horns and deal with the situation.

In my early days at the sheriff's office, I decided this was panning out to be a fun and exciting career. I was able to respond to more than just animal calls. I had the ability to respond to a couple of natural deaths to learn about how to handle those situations, as well as domestic violence calls. I also assisted one of the local police agencies with a suicide. It was an unpleasant situation, watching as the officers dealt with the family and then waiting for the coroner. Everything was going well, and I was enjoying the experience—until October 1995. That time will live in my mind forever.

Reality Sets In

One day in October 1995, I went to my office and started my daily routine. I checked for any voicemails that may have come through or any paperwork from other deputies who may have picked up stray dogs. I fed, watered, and cleaned out the kennels while the dogs enjoyed some time in the outside run. Once this was completed, I responded to the dispatch center to check for any pending calls. When I walked into dispatch, I noticed everyone appeared to be crying or upset, and I knew something bad had happened; I just didn't know what it was right away.

I was caught at the door by the on-duty sergeant and told I was going to be in a deputy role for the day, taking calls for service as help was needed on the road. All animal issues would have to wait unless someone was getting attacked. The sergeant appeared to have tears in his eyes and was more serious than normal.

I asked what was going on and was told one of our deputies appeared to have killed himself while on shift during the night. This made me take a step back for a moment. I was not quite sure what to say, especially after I found out the deputy's name: Ken. I had a hard time imagining him doing such a thing. He had such a love for life and for his wife. He volunteered on his days off for kid organizations, even though he did not have any children. He was an avid outdoorsman, and he enjoyed the job. It was rare not to see him smile during his shift.

I was told Ken had been guarding a crime scene during the overnight hours. It was considered a possible arson because there were no reports of fires in the area or anything to ignite a house, such as a lightning strike; it was too cold and had been a very wet year. The homeowner was reported to be out of the state, as this was a vacation cabin home and occupied for only three months out of the year during the summer. In the early morning hours, dispatch had been trying to get in contact with him on the radio to check his status without success. Checking the status of officers was a common task by dispatch every hour when it was a quiet shift. When the day shift started, Gary was dispatched to check on Ken as soon as he called into service. This is where Ken was found unconscious, with a gunshot wound to the head. The gunshot appeared to be self-inflicted.

By the time I got into dispatch, the investigation was just beginning, and investigators had not put two and two together yet. Later in the morning, I was instructed to take some water to Gary, who was still on the scene and had been there for several hours already. Gary was going to be there for several more hours; he was guarding Ken's body and had to wait for the county coroner to arrive on the scene. It was unknown how long this wait would be. On my drive to the location, I thought nothing much about the situation. I just couldn't believe what was happening. I really did not know what to think.

I made the final turn onto a dirt road and continued to Gary's location. As he saw me approaching, he walked quickly toward my vehicle, trying to catch me before I could see anything more than I had to. Unfortunately, he was not quick enough, and I continued to drive over to him. The body wasn't completely covered. The wind had blown the blanket off while Gary was on his way toward me.

This was not the first dead body I had seen during my time in the department; I had seen a few. But it was my first deceased officer—a friend, and a brother. I silently handed Gary the bottles of water, turned, and walked away. Neither one of us could really say anything. I didn't know if I should. What I did know was this: cops don't show emotion in front of anyone else. We are supposed to be tough and able to handle any situation no matter what; this is what we were taught in the academy and what we learned from watching seasoned deputies.

As I walked away, it struck me that Ken was the second deputy I'd met on my first day, and he was also the one deceased on the ground. I thought back to that day. He had been friendly and told me not to end up becoming the "old cranky guy" like so many others in the department. He was a friend to everyone and was always willing to cover calls when someone needed help or to have a barbecue on his days off so we could all get to know each other a little better. He believed the department was a family and that we should treat each other as such. He made sure that happened.

As I walked back to my patrol car, I could hardly breathe. Just over a year on the job and I saw a coworker lying dead on the ground, and everyone was still thinking it was due to suicide; this is what scared the living shit out of me. That could have been any of us. I still didn't believe he had killed himself, and I refused to believe that. As I was driving away from the scene, I remember thinking back on my time in the police academy. I remember all the scenarios we ran through, the investigations that were talked about, and the pictures of homicide victims. However, we never had to deal with the loss of a coworker. Some things just aren't taught or talked about in our training. This is the stuff that is kept quiet because they don't want to scare the recruits. Maybe they should have made us aware. I believe the likelihood of on-duty officer deaths is something every recruit needs to know. It's something that no one can ever truly prepare themselves for; but it would help to at least know of its possibility and how to deal with it.

When I returned to the office, I was teamed up with another deputy. We had gone through the same academy together and were now working for the same department. He had the same look on his face everyone else did. I'm guessing I had that look as well: disbelief, fear, and not knowing what to say, think, or even do.

As the day continued, we were taking calls for service and handling situations as they came up. This kept us busy for the full shift. A couple of hours into the shift, everyone was advised the detectives had learned that Ken had been murdered; he did not take his own life. We were also informed his weapons were missing. All firearms were gone—the one on his duty belt and the shotgun out of the vehicle. The suspect had taken his time to figure out how to get those weapons unlocked and leave enough time to escape.

Great! Now, there was some turd running around in the woods with more guns, and we had no idea where the hell they were. The real search began: looking for the piece of shit who shot a deputy guarding a crime scene. As the shift ended, we were sent home. This is where reality set in, and the fact a deputy was killed in the line of duty in this county really hit home. I'd been a cop for just over a year, and this tragedy has already happened. What else was to come? How could I do this knowing the potential threat I was facing? Yes, this scared the shit out of me, and I lay awake that night wondering if I really was capable of doing this job, if I really wanted to do this job, if my life was worth losing for people I didn't know or for those who may not like me because I was a cop.

This was not like the television shows I watched growing up as a kid, things I didn't hear about on the news or more than likely didn't pay attention to. I had watched many around me hurting because of this loss, questioning whether they could continue and worrying about their families if something were to happen to them—all the same thoughts I had. I am sure they were lying awake, too.

I was able to get a couple of hours of sleep that night. When I woke up the next morning, I had made the decision that the job was worth continuing. I had decided quitting this career would be a disgrace to those who'd lost their fight in the line of duty. I wasn't going to let some piece of shit scumbag get into my head. This was the career path I chose, and if that was the outcome, then it was meant to be. Hell, I could be killed driving to the grocery store. Nothing made this different. Up to this point, I had seen a few deaths and understood that people die. I would just try to make sure I kept myself alive and helped protect those I worked with and those around me. So off to work I went, wearing that uniform proudly and ready for whatever was to come.

When I arrived at work, I was advised I would be spending my day at the crime scene trying to locate any evidence of where the suspect may have gone. I was in charge of leading a team of civilians with metal detectors and watching over their safety. What I didn't realize was just how close to the suspect we were about to be. When I arrived at the scene, the volunteer team was ready to go. They had already been advised as to what they were searching for and what to do if anything was located.

If anything of question was found, the volunteer would raise their arm, and I would place a little locator flag in the area where it would be further searched at a later time. We were out for several hours searching a hillside on the property near and around the arson scene. A couple hours in, another officer in the distance located a house that appeared to have been broken into. They then heard noise from inside.

As I looked over my right shoulder, I realized I was looking right at the house. There were five windows facing the civilians and myself about thirty yards away. We had been completely exposed for the last couple of hours. Detectives already had information about the homeowners being away for the winter, so nobody should have been in the house. A nearby SWAT team came to assist from a small town within the county. They were able to assemble quickly and make entry right away. Dispatch advised there to be radio silence; nobody was to talk on the radio who was not part of that team. Also, we all wanted to hear what was found.

After several seconds, the radio silence was broken by the call of one of the SWAT officers stating there was a gunshot heard from an upstairs bedroom in the residence and they were forcing entry. The next radio transmission was the team leader advising to send an ambulance for a single, self-inflicted gunshot to the head of the suspect. The suspect had shot himself; he took the coward's way out. Many of us were angry and had wanted retribution. He took that away from us by taking his own life. What a piece of shit.

Don't get me wrong. We wanted him dead. We had hoped he would be taken out during a gunfight, but we would have been just as happy to see him die in prison instead. By taking his own life, he robbed us of an explanation of why he felt the need to kill a deputy—and a sense of closure.

When the SWAT team exited the house, they advised where the bedroom was located. As stated before, several of us had been in view of this piece of shit, including all the civilians. It struck us all very quickly that he could have taken another shot at any one of us wearing a uniform to scare those of us in his line of view at first. We realized that if he really wanted to go out in a blaze of glory, that would have been the way to do it: start shooting at those he could see from the upstairs bedroom of the house.

However, it was over, and there was nothing more to worry about. The most likely suspect in Ken's murder was dead. After everyone started breathing again, the search continued to find more evidence. There was still more information to be obtained. A different team was inside the house when the coroner arrived. It did make me realize how important it was to keep my head on a swivel and always— I mean *always*—be aware of my surroundings.

This wasn't the academy anymore, and if someone took a shot, it wasn't just going to be with paint and leave a welt. It was going to be permanent damage. This definitely changed me and the way I looked at officer safety. Sometimes, I guess that's what it takes. From that moment on, I put the experience to use.

During the next couple of days, those of us working at the department were told they found a diary left by the suspect. Those of us who wanted to see it were able to review the copies made by the detectives. Of course, I wanted to know what had been in the mind of such a coward. The diary rambled on about a demon telling the suspect to kill people. Not just anybody, though. The suspect wanted to kill a police officer.

The diary went back several months, which gave the suspect time to plan his actions. He knew our department was small and lacked manpower, and he believed those two factors would make it easier for him to carry out his plans. The suspect had been performing surveillance on our department, thus knowing there were only a couple of deputies who worked the night shift at the time. He also knew, through watching television shows, that a deputy would be placed at an arson to guard the scene while the department put together a plan of action for investigating such a crime.

Within the last few pages of his diary, he began rambling on about how he was going to set a house on fire because it was what the demons were telling him to do. On the day this all started, he set the house fire to look like an obvious arson. He did not want to make it look like an accident or act of nature. If it appeared to be an accident, a wiring issue, or an act of God, nobody would remain at the scene.

He also had it mapped out, sketched by hand, which house he was going to burn; he knew the area was full of summertime owners and that they would be gone during October when it began to get cold. While the house was burning, he was watching the firefighters trying to put it out. He wrote about how good it felt to set the fire and how excited he felt knowing his desire to kill an officer was about to be satisfied. The suspect knew the house next to the one he burned was also vacant, and that was where he would hide. He described how he broke in and which door he left open for a quick escape after the fire was set. He enjoyed watching the firefighters work to put out the fire, along with the deputies placed in the roadway to block traffic.

Once the emergency vehicles left the scene, the suspect wrote that he noticed one patrol vehicle sitting in the driveway of the burned residence. This was his cue to take action. He waited until the early hours of the morning when the deputy was getting tired and focusing on his report. It was still dark outside, and it was easy to move around in the darkness without being seen. He just had to stay quiet enough to avoid being heard, as well.

He walked to the back of the patrol vehicle, got on his hands and knees, and crawled around the vehicle to the driver's side. As he approached the driver's side door, he got his shotgun ready. He knew he would have to be quick in order to make sure his plans worked. He opened the door and immediately placed the shotgun under Ken's chin and pulled the trigger. Ken had no time to react and was killed instantly.

The suspect wrote about how the killing quieted the demon in his head for a short time. However, it also excited him, making him want to kill more. He knew more deputies would show up on the scene. In the last pages of his diary, he wrote down how he wanted to kill more but couldn't, as too many had shown up at once. He was not expecting such a huge police presence the following day.

He figured there would be a few, and he would be able to shoot them before he was found. But with how many deputies and officers from surrounding towns showed up to the scene to help, he decided to stay in the vacant home and continue hiding. This was where his writings stopped. He added no more information before he took his own life. He did apologize to his mother multiple times in the diary, letting her know he would be in the news and that would be the last time she would see him. Reading his diary brought up anger and a lot of other emotions. I now understood the evil that was out there and what I would be facing moving forward in this career. Up until now, this was the stuff I'd only heard about in the news or read in stories. Until you actually see it and live it, it is easy to say it's the kind of thing you hope to never have to face.

Several days later, we were heading to a funeral—the funeral of a friend, coworker, and brother; it was a very somber moment, and when true reality set in, so did the pain of the final goodbye. I rode with two other deputies; we did some talking on the way about things we remembered while working with our friend. The procession was long. There were law enforcement officers who had come from all over the country, officers we had never met, and departments we had never heard of. The line of patrol vehicles seemed to go on for an eternity. It was truly impressive to see the outpouring of support for our department and for Ken's family.

To be honest, the service is quite a blur to me; I don't remember a lot of it. I think some of the reason is that I was so busy trying not to lose it myself, trying to maintain that level of toughness expected—being stoic, I guess one could say. What I do remember is the pain and sadness everyone was going through, especially Ken's wife. The other memory I will always have is the playing of "Taps" on the bugle, and "Amazing Grace" and another song I did not know being played on the bagpipes.

After the funeral was over, we all had to get back to normal, dealing with the everyday grind, taking calls for service, and performing my animal control duties. Contacting pet owners about their animal licenses was getting old after a year, although the people I dealt with were nice—mostly. I did contact plenty of people who were pissed off by my reminding them about such a petty thing, too.

These people would threaten to call the sheriff and complain because I was bothering them. They were the same people who would receive a ticket after their multiple warnings; only so many chances are given. I put up with no shit from anybody. They could tell the judge how much bullshit it was they received a ticket for not licensing their dogs and why they didn't think it was necessary.

The Power of a Single Word

The nice thing was I never had to go to court during the time I worked as animal control. Nobody ever fought their tickets. They would just pay and get their dog licenses. The day did come when a position for a road deputy opened, and I put in for it. I had to go through the full hiring process again. Even though I already worked for the department and had completed a polygraph and background, I had to repeat it all because the new sheriff had his own agenda. When the results of my polygraph came back, it showed I had passed and answered all the questions honestly. However, the sheriff decided he didn't like the way I worded the reason I left a previous job several years prior.

He told me that since I hadn't put that I was "fired" and used that exact word for the reason I was leaving, I had lied on my application and therefore would be terminated at the end of the year, which was three months away. He told me he was going to fire me at the end of the year but couldn't lose the position right then. *What the hell did that mean?* I'd never heard of such a thing before, being told you are going to be fired several months before it was to happen. How strange!

After thinking about being terminated in three months for something so petty as a word, I knew something was not right, and there was more to the reason he was waiting so long. So, with that in mind, I decided to go and talk to a lawyer. I needed to have a better answer than the bullshit the sheriff had told me. Apparently, I chose the right lawyer. I found out this lawyer had a hate for the sheriff from his time at another agency, and he was more than happy to help me out with this issue. The lawyer wrote a letter to the sheriff stating the cause for termination was not legal and that a lawsuit would be pending if my status was not changed. I found out someone can be fired for no reason at all; but not using a particular word when explaining why one left a job was not a legal reason, and nor was it legal for me to be expected to work for several more months knowing I was going to be terminated. The letter was sent to the sheriff, and the real truth finally came out: there was no opening for another deputy position. The sheriff knew I would apply. He was looking to find a reason to fire me because they were terminating the actual position I was working. Laying me off would mean they would have to leave the position unfilled until I was offered the position back first.

Since I was not part of the "good ol' boys' club," he was looking for any reason possible to terminate me. He thought he had found a good one. Unfortunately for him, he found out I was no dummy, and he was performing illegal acts with his cause for termination. After he agreed to change my status, I informed him I was going to resign at the end of the year. I no longer wanted to work for this asshole. I was sure he would pull something else, trying to get rid of me.

This is when I learned what it was like to work for a sheriff's department, and I didn't like the uneasy feeling of knowing I could be fired for no reason at any given time. But I continued working my job as normal until the end of the year. In January of 1996, I was unemployed again and looking for a city police department to work for. It wasn't until October of that year when I was hired by a small gambling town—and I mean *small*. The town was one square mile and had a living population of about 1,500 people, but there was a constant flow of tourists in town every day. I had applied to several places before being offered this position. At the time, every police department wanted an associate degree to even be considered for hiring. Hell, there really was no requirement on the degree; it could have been a degree in underwater basket weaving as far as they cared. So, in August 1996, I started my college education. Little did I know I would be offered a job two months later. Many adventures were ahead for me, and it turned out to be a blast.

Part IV: Moving On

"Cops work for a cause, not applause."

—Unknown

The First Year

When I started in this one-square-mile town, I had also just started taking college courses a few months prior. I was already certified within the state to become a police officer, so I could go right into a twelve-week field-training program.

My training sergeant knew this little gambling town well. He gave me a tour of the casinos, showed me where the locals hung out, and introduced me to several of the residents. I met the employees and, most importantly, the security officers. I say "most importantly" here because I would later learn how closely we worked with them and the riff-raff who would visit the casinos.

For the first few weeks, I wasn't allowed to do much of anything, such as using the radio, talking to people on calls, or driving the police car. I was only to meet and greet people, watch as my sergeant/trainer took calls, and learn how he responded to different people depending on the situation and how they treated him. I would also have to sit around while he wrote his reports and then read them when he was done.

While waiting for the sarge to write his reports, I would be reviewing handwritten booking reports, search warrants, and arrest warrants written by other officers on previous cases. This review would help me understand what was required for each of those documents. I did learn a lot later, understanding what and what not to write. I also learned there are a lot of officers who simply cannot write a sentence.

With my luck, I had a sergeant who passed enough gas to fuel the car. He was a nasty bastard, and I had to ride with him for several weeks. His favorite thing to do was lock the windows, which then wouldn't allow me to roll the powered window down, and fart. For the first several weeks, this was an added challenge I would have to work with; I truly believe there was damage done to my nose because of this guy. I kept telling him he would regret it one day, and he would just laugh and continue driving through town, not allowing me to roll down the window.

Keep in mind that, at the time, it was common for new officers to be treated this way. They were messed with and hazed into their career. It was okay to swear at them or ask, "What the fuck are you doing?" Nowadays, if you talk to a new officer this way, a complaint will be made, and the

74

training officer will get demoted, written up, or even terminated. New officers back then were also referred to as a "boot" or "rookie" for the first several weeks of field training. You weren't called by name because it was not known whether you'd make it to the end or not.

During these first two weeks in FTO, I kept my nose clean. I stayed out of trouble, as no actual calls ever came up. We had some verbal domestic arguments between husbands and wives, actual domestic cases involving assault, a few thefts from the casinos, and a couple of drug and warrant arrests. So, I reviewed plenty of documents and learned how this department performed arrest control tactics. I was also required to learn the street names and the block numbers throughout the town.

Every once in a while, the sarge would stop the car mid-block and ask where we were, what street we were on, which hundred block, or what streets we were between. If I didn't get it right, he would make me get out of the vehicle, walk to the street sign, and yell out our location so he could hear it. For a bonus, he would hit the lights and siren to attract attention, letting everyone know I was a rookie and had no clue where I was. By the time I completed those first two weeks, I had the town's streets down pat. There was no street I couldn't locate. Of course, we are talking about a small town that was somewhat easy to figure out.

After getting through that first phase, I was able to move on and become more involved with the calls, taking on the lead officer role when interviewing suspects, victims, and witnesses. I would write police reports when calls were completed and make arrests when required. If a ticket was issued, the sergeant would walk me through the process and provide direction on proper charges for the suspect, whether for an arrest or a traffic citation. It wasn't until later in training that I would learn how to complete paperwork for a felony crime—only because we didn't deal with any felonies up to that point.

This field training was a new concept; my training with the sheriff's department had been old-school and less extensive. Their approach was simple: *Here's a badge and car keys. Now, get to work.* You would just learn as you went along, taking advice from the other deputies. But here, I was really learning a lot and enjoying the training I was receiving.

There were not many officers in this small department. We had a chief who was hardly ever seen, and his wife, who was one of the officers. There was a deputy chief, whom we saw every once in a while when he wasn't attending meetings for the chief. There were also two patrol sergeants, an executive sergeant (the only person he supervised was the detective), and twelve patrol officers.

We also had an animal control officer who was so busy taking care of the city's computer issues he was hardly ever around or available to do the job he was actually hired to do. I found out very quickly how much our schedules could change if an officer called in sick or quit and moved on to another department. This would place everyone on twelve-hour shifts until the sick officer came back to work or the position was filled.

Getting back to field training, this was where I learned that I would much rather work for a city department than a county department. I wasn't worried about my job being in jeopardy if the chief were to resign his position. We kept ourselves busy, and my sergeant always found something for me to do. Every day started out with making sure his equipment was in the vehicle before mine, meaning I would have to unload his personal vehicle and place his duty bag and gear into the car for him.

I would also make sure my boots were polished before we hit the road, because he would mark me down for appearance if I had a scratch on my boots. We never really dealt with any serious crimes during field training. The majority were misdemeanors, casino issues at the local level (thefts, assaults, etc.), some drugs (mostly methamphetamines and some marijuana), and traffic issues when none of that other stuff was going on. We had the occasional domestic violence calls, but only a couple necessitated an arrest. I had no idea I would have to become a marriage counselor for people who hadn't quite figured out how to be adults. I also learned how to be a family counselor for those with kids who couldn't be controlled.

The biggest problem when dealing with kids whose parents called us was the parents. They would not discipline their kids but had no problem telling the kids I would arrest them if they didn't behave. As irritating as this was, I was still in training, so I had to deal with these issues professionally and make sure the kids understood their parents were the adults. I had to make it clear that the kids were to listen to what they were told.

Keep in mind, this was a different time, and laws consisting of stricter enforcement around domestic violence and child abuse were being implemented. Kids were being told in school that their parents were not allowed to spank them and that the kids had a right to call the police for abuse if they were physically disciplined. It was hard, then, to make kids listen to their parents; and the frustrated parents would call us to come and be the bad guys and discipline their children.

I remember how I was dealt with as a child. When I did something wrong, the belt and a wooden spoon were the most common weapons of choice for spankings. Now, in the mid-1990s, someone who spanked their child was bound to have the police called, and the Department of Social Services was contacted because of potential levels of violence that may have been used against children. What people did not understand was that while they had the right to discipline their children, they just couldn't use such things as wooden spoons, belts, or paddles anymore.

It was right around this time when domestic violence laws became stricter, as well. The courts did not just want a simple separation of both parties; the courts wanted a full charge of domestic violence if there was an obvious crime committed beyond the normal yelling at each other. Gone were the days of two young people having money issues and trying to raise a family, getting into an argument, and one pushing the other out of the way. Or the wife finding out her husband has been cheating and slapping him in the face out of disgust. We used to just separate these couples and get one out of the situation until things calmed down.

Too many times, it couldn't be determined as to who made the first contact, so both parties would be arrested. We would just let the courts sort it out. The biggest problem was having to respond to the same couple time after time, with the male being the one arrested every single time. In these situations, it's hard not to lose empathy for a victim who keeps accepting the abuser back in when help has been offered every damn time.

During this time, couples learned that one would go to jail if the other called the cops and demanded this to happen, even if nothing physical happened—or the one reporting the incident would be arrested instead. This is where the resisting arrest would start.

I finally hit the last two weeks of my field training, and I was put back with my first training officer/sergeant, and it was time for payback for being forced to sit in his stench with the windows locked and the vehicle moving.

This was during my test-out phase, the last two weeks, when I took calls and the sergeant would just observe, even when I was waiting for my cover car to arrive. This was also in the middle of December when the temperature was about ten degrees outside.

The first night back to start my work week, and what the sergeant didn't know was I had prepared for his smelly ass. The night before, I had a few beers and ate some pickled eggs. The "boil up" to the shift was perfect for payback. The shift started at 10 p.m. I loaded the patrol vehicle with my equipment, and we hit the road to do some patrolling, making sure there were no accidents or issues in the casinos. We got into the car and were driving around for about thirty minutes when he said he wanted to drive because he was getting tired, and it would wake him up a bit.

Knowing what he was really wanting to do, I agreed to let him drive. Not long after, I watched him lock the windows on the car. He knew I wouldn't open the door while he was driving because of how cold it was. Well, I was prepared for him and was just waiting for it. Sure as shit, I could smell the nastiness in the car. While trying to push the button to get the window down, I told him, "It's time for payback," and released something worse than he had. The problem was between both of us. It was far beyond what he could even stand.

The next thing I knew, he slammed the patrol car into park, and we both dived out, gagging and trying not to throw up right in the middle of the block of casinos where everyone was watching. I am sure it was a sight to see, and people were wondering what the hell was wrong with us. After several minutes of laughing and trying to breathe again, we got back into the car, rolled all the windows down, and had to go switch the car out for another vehicle because the stench was so strong neither could stand to be in the car. We parked this one and left it for the day shift officer (the day sergeant) without saying anything in the morning.

I know it's not nice, but what do you do? My direct sergeant told me to, and we must follow direct orders. End result: this did not happen again. The lesson had been taught and learned, and the rest of my two weeks in FTO were odor-free and smooth sailing, except for those we would arrest who hadn't bathed in God only knows how long.

At the end of 1996, I had completed field training, even after almost killing my sergeant in chemical warfare. This was just in time for Christmas and to work my first holiday shift. It was the beginning of working many holidays for me; I really enjoyed the holiday pay and the building-up of time to take off later. My first Christmas was pretty quiet for the most part; the worst we had to deal with were some traffic stops due to boredom and having nothing better to do. The chief and his wife brought food to the department so we could celebrate, as well; we didn't go hungry.

My first year was full of excitement—dealing with burglary and assault cases, learning about casino laws, and plenty of training. Some of my favorite training was learning about motorcycle gangs; this was important because we had a motorcycle rally in the town every year in August. The rally would happen the week after Sturgis, so we knew when it was coming and could be prepared.

Also, during my first year, I became a member of the SWAT team, going through even more training and exciting call-outs. This kept the adrenaline pumping every time we would get called in; it also kept me from drinking alcohol for several years to come, because I was on-call 24/7—we never knew when we would be needed, day or night. It was very exciting to know something cool could happen at any time. I didn't want to miss a call because I had been drinking, and we had to get permission to be off-call, leaving the team one officer short if there was an emergency.

This first year is when I had my first real fight with a suspect. Now, I am not talking about a simple resisting charge or someone just trying to keep from getting arrested. I am talking about a true knockdown, drag-out fight. My sergeant and I responded to a casino during a Wednesday karaoke night where a known individual was hanging out and had a warrant for his arrest. I will call him Jason,. His story will continue throughout my career. We approached Jason and advised him that he had a warrant and needed to come with us.

He told us to go away because he was singing next, and he would have to be physically moved from his chair. I believe his exact words were, "Get the fuck away from me. I am singing next. You are going to have to drag me out kicking and singing to keep me from getting on that stage." I thought, "Damn, is he looking to get made from this small-ass town?" I even asked him, "Do you think singing karaoke in this casino is going to make you famous?" Then my sergeant stepped in and told him, "Let's go, Elvis. Get your ass out of that chair." Jason was a feisty fucker. He was skinny and wiry and had construction-worker strength.

Well, we began to physically move Jason from his chair, and that's when his fists and feet started flying. He was doing everything he could to keep from getting placed into custody, and with that, we fought back. I got clocked in the face a couple of times, he was kicking the shit out of Sarge, and we were giving it right back to him. Tables were getting knocked over, along with people in their chairs. There were some glasses broken and blood spraying. We did have him on the ground for a short time, but he managed to get back on his feet and square off again.

My sergeant and I decided tackling him would be a good idea, and so we did—right over the top of a table. Our tackle broke the shit out of the table, and we all went to the ground again. We ended up on the floor, Jason lying on his stomach, where he decided to lock his hands together underneath his body. He was a strong fucker, and we tried several times to break his grip to get him handcuffed. Eventually, the batons came out and were used to break the hold. Batons work great for leverage. They pry at the elbow and push away from the body. Not only does this hurt, but it is effective.

Sarge used a couple of baton strikes to the back of Jason's thigh. Although he would yell "ouch," he still did not want to go to jail. He really wanted to sing that one last song before he had to leave for the night. I have to say this was one time I began to worry about my own safety. Once the batons came out, the crowd of his friends began to circle around us and were getting closer. I was thinking I was going to get a boot to the face and was just hoping it didn't happen. I remember yelling several times, "Get back" and "Back the fuck up." Thankfully, the rest of the crowd listened and came no closer.

After what seemed like forever, we were finally able to get Jason in custody. All three of us were bleeding, bruised, and tired. In the end, he lost and went to jail without being able to sing on that stage for his big karaoke event. This all happened in a time before video recording on cell phones, personal recording devices, and clear security camera footage. But I would have liked to see the surveillance recording, even if it was kind of fuzzy and out of focus. I know it would have been entertaining to watch.

It was also around this time that I had to respond to my first fatal traffic accident. The call was in the county, but since the accident was about a mile out of town, we went ahead and responded to the scene. When I arrived, I noticed it was a single motorcycle accident. The driver appeared to have been way over the speed limit and laid the bike down. This was a guess based on the skid marks he left and how far the bike continued to slide after it laid over. I noticed a helmet stuck between two posts in the guardrail but thought nothing of it; however, none of us saw a body right away.

With the skid marks on the ground, we were assuming the victim continued farther than the bike and ended up down the hill somewhere in the field. I decided to go and check out the helmet as part of the wreckage. The opening of the helmet was facing away from the road, and toward the field, so nobody really paid attention or even thought about what would be found next. Of course, I had to look at the open end of the helmet.

Well, there was a face staring back at me; the victim's head was still in the helmet. It was dark out, as the accident had happened at night. In the outskirts of the town, there was no lighting near the roadway. I thought to myself, "Well, fuck. We are going to be here a while." At about this time, the State Patrol arrived on the scene and asked what we had. I proceeded to let him know we had the head, which was still in the helmet, but had no idea where the body was. Of course, by doing that, I'd opened myself up to be told to start looking for the rest of the victim. Two county deputies and I began searching the field on the other side of the guardrail.

As we walked down the hill, all three of us noticed, at about the same time, a lump of something in the grass. It was the rest of the victim. He was not easy to see at first because, besides it being nighttime, he was wearing a dark jacket and chaps. There he was, headless and mangled. One of the deputies looked at both of us and said, "I guess his leather and helmet couldn't save him on this one. Lost his head over the whole situation...literally."

This was my first fatal traffic accident, and it was interesting to watch how the state patrol worked the scene, taking measurements and diagramming the accident. I did learn a lot that night— even the fact that not even a helmet and leather can save someone on a motorcycle. After the state patrol took measurements and completed calculations, it was determined the victim was driving at approximately 100 miles per hour on the curvy roads. Definitely a recipe for disaster.

The SWAT Years

Within the same timeframe, the department decided to put together a SWAT team. Those who were interested had to go through an interview and a physical test. The test was like any other; I had to complete a 1.5-mile run, 40 sit-ups, and 25 pushups. I was in better shape back then, so it was really no problem to complete. After the testing, six of us were chosen to move forward. We all had to go through a one-week training program that was intense. If you thought you were in shape, this was going to show you weren't in shape.

We had several guys who didn't make it through training. They had a difficult time with some of the tasks. This town was in the mountains and surrounded by rough terrain of hills and mountainsides—so we had to train in the same type of environment. We went on daily runs over hills on the outskirts of town. We didn't want the locals to see what we were actually doing. We spent several hours at the range training on tactical entries of different objects, such as houses, buses, and schools.

We would belly-crawl through fields, like we were making a low-profile approach to locations, and run some more with all our gear on and carrying our weapons. We would run into the firing range and have to shoot a series of targets. During one of our low crawls, the detective and detective sergeant in charge of this training, both previous Marines, decided it would be fun to start one morning with a belly-crawl around a building after it had rained the night before.

What they didn't tell us was there was a nice body of water we had to go through behind the building. If we were not willing to go through, we were not going to continue as members of the team. We don't back out of a situation because we don't want to get wet or dirty; however, we had no idea of their intentions until we crawled our asses to the back side of the building.

The lead guy of this mission came to a stop and was going to find a way around this body of mud water, but the two in charge caught him and told him to continue through, and the rest would follow. Like sheep, we all did what we were told and belly-crawled through this mud puddle for about fifty yards, and it was fucking cold. By the time we all got through the other side, there wasn't one of us who didn't have the uncontrollable shakes. We were soaked to the bone and ready to kick the shit out of the two in charge.

Lucky for them, we were all too focused on trying to warm up. They sent us all back to the police department, where we were able to change and get into some dry clothes before the rest of the training continued for the day. We were all glad when it was over—forty hours of training completed in four ten-hour days. It was brutal, but we all survived.

As we went through a small graduation ceremony, the chief made an appearance (it was one of the few times we actually saw him) to give us our certificates and take photos with the team. In the end, we had a total of six team members ready to go. Going through something like this really does teach you how to be a team player. Without one, the rest of the team is incapacitated or does not exist.

Following the forty hours of training, it was time to get down to business, and the real training began. We pulled a lot of overtime over the next several months to be ready for anything that could happen. Once our leaders felt the rest of the team was ready for deployment, we mainly focused on executing search and arrest warrants, along with drug raids. Over the next ten years, we completed several high-risk warrants: two were for homicide suspects (one homicide in our town and one wanted from another state), about ten barricaded subjects due to domestic violence situations, and a large manhunt in another part of the state.

I'm not sure how, but we were getting noticed by other agencies in a good way. We had been asked by other agencies to respond to assist on call-outs. One was in an area called the Four Corners, where four states bordered each other: Colorado, New Mexico, Arizona, and Utah.

This was a multi-agency manhunt looking for three suspects who were wanted for the murder of a law enforcement officer. The agency involved had called our chief and asked for us to join them, and we were ready to go in a matter of two hours. When we arrived at the command post on the Colorado side, it was late, and the search was ending for the day, so we were put up in an area hotel for the night to get some rest. As we woke up the next morning, we responded to the command post and were placed on an area highway where Colorado and New Mexico met. It was the middle of summer, so of course it was hotter than hell, and we were dressed in all black.

Apparently, our team leader thought we were going to be working in the dark or something and didn't wait to find out what we were doing first. This was our post for the day. We were to check vehicles coming and going to make sure nobody was hiding or being stored in a vehicle to escape being caught. Throughout the day, we searched hundreds of vehicles, including food delivery vehicles like Schwann's. This turned out to be a good contact.

The driver was very cooperative and friendly. He wasn't upset at all with being held up. In fact, before he left, he decided our team needed ice cream and popsicles. As he was pulling these items out of his truck, someone mentioned trying to keep everything from melting, since the temperature was nearing one hundred degrees.

Apparently, the vehicle behind him overheard the conversation and pulled out a cooler with ice packs for us to use to keep our ice cream cold. They were disposable, so we wouldn't have to figure out how to return these items. The Schwann's driver refused to take any form of payment from us. By the end of the day, the whole team was tired from the heat and glad it was over. We still had another day to go and were afraid we would be doing the same thing all over again.

As we responded to the command post on day two, we were happy to hear doing road duty was not on our agenda for the day. Instead, we were going to be searching surrounding areas. When I say surrounding areas, I am talking about cornfields and cliffs. The fields had already been mowed down, so it made things easier to see farther.

What we didn't know was we would be doing this by helicopter, which excited most of us; however, our team leader was not happy about it at all—he was afraid of flying. We were bused to the location of the chopper, which was a military bird with dual rotors. As we all climbed in, I sat in the seat to the far right, facing forward. Our team lead sat across from me while facing the rear. I was pretty sure he was either going to piss himself or vomit once we started flying.

Of course, I had to pick the seat that wasn't bolted on one side; they called it the gunner's seat because it would swing out to the right of the chopper and hang over the edge. My team lead told me that wasn't allowed, so I had to place my foot on the seat in front of me, our team lead's seat, in order to keep from swinging out. This was even harder whenever the pilot would bank to the right; the bird would lean enough that my seat wanted to just swivel right on out there. It was quite a trip, flying over the fields and being able to see as much as we did.

One of the two times we landed for a search was for an underground bunker found in the middle of a cornfield. As we touched down, our team made its way over to the bunker and carefully opened the door. Prior to opening, we had discussed tossing in a couple of flash-bangs just in case there was someone hiding down there, but we decided it might be overkill. When we opened the door to the bunker, two other officers took a quick peek inside. It appeared nobody was hiding there, so a thorough search was performed.

As the two officers came out, they advised it was a good thing flash bangs were not used since there were three cases of dynamite at the bottom of the steps, two fifty-gallon tanks full of kerosene, and gas cans full of diesel fuel that could have been a mess. We later found out the dynamite was legally owned by the landowner—for what reason, we really never knew. But it could have been a real bad ending to the day. After finishing up, we all loaded back onto the helicopter and took off again.

Our second landing was on the top of a cliff's edge. We were to climb down the cliff wall to check out what looked to be a cave in the face of the cliff. As we unloaded, we made our way to the edge of the cliff and began working our way down to the cave. Once we were all down, we went back to the cave, which didn't go too deep into the hillside, but just deep enough for someone to hide if they wanted.

It did seem there had been someone staying in the cave at some point; there was a small fire pit with food wrappers lying around it. I am guessing bears don't start fires. It appeared that whoever had been there hadn't been inside for quite some time. The food wrappers were slightly faded, and the ashes in the firepit were blown around. We made our way back to the top of the cliff, loaded back onto the helicopter, and flew around for a while longer. We noticed there were several caves along the cliff's edge, but we couldn't fly down low enough to really get a look and didn't have time to search all of them. We headed back to the command post to rethink our strategy.

After about an hour, it was decided to use a smaller, open-bellied helicopter to take a closer look at the caves on the side of the cliffs where we were. Having a glass bottom made it easier to see in all different directions. Sgt. Riker, one of the teams' leaders, and I chose to take the flight along that cliff wall. I had done fine in the big chopper, so this should've been no problem at all.

The flight was smooth. There was no difference between this helicopter and the last until we hit the cliffs and canyons. Once this thing went out over the canyon, you could feel it drop like a rollercoaster ride, and my stomach hit my throat. I thought I was going to vomit and tried really hard not to. Of course, being the tough guy I thought I was, I said nothing and just rode it out for the next two hours.

This bird had a glass bottom, so we were able to look below us and around us, which was pretty cool. We were also able to get a closer look at the caves we had seen earlier. We had to map out which ones appeared to have been visited by humans at some point so other teams could go out at a later time and complete a search on all of them. After a couple of hours, Sgt. Riker and I were taken back to the command post. It was determined the searches were going to be stopped after that day because local forecasters were expecting bad weather, and those in charge didn't want to put anybody in danger of getting lost or hurt. We made our way back home that night. It was a long, exhausting couple of days, but well worth the experience and the confidence placed in us by the other agencies who'd asked for our help.

Of the many search warrants we executed over the years, only one made me stop in my tracks upon entry and truly feel bad about it. This was during the winter, and it was very cold outside, but we needed to execute this search warrant due to the amount of drugs we knew were inside the house. It was the only time we knew there were fewer people inside, as well.

The house was always busy, with people coming and going as the dealers would bring back large quantities of meth. The only timeframe we had was around three in the morning when we knew there would be no more visitors. My goggles fogged up once the team made entry into the residence, caused by going from cold air to warm. The house was nice and toasty inside. I couldn't see shit for a short time. The department didn't want to foot the bill for goggles that didn't fog up, so all I could make out were silhouettes of furniture and people.

I was the first officer in the residence, and I had my weapon up and ready because we knew the residents of the house were known to be armed themselves. I could see outlines of two people on the ground entering into a hallway. I just couldn't see if they were male or female, adults or children. I immediately yelled at these two to stay on the ground and show their hands, of course hoping neither of them were armed. I stopped and held on to these two while the rest of the team secured the rest of the house.

As my goggles started to clear up, I realized I had a female and a boy, approximately eight years old, placed on the ground and held at gunpoint. Once I could see again, the look on the boy's face said everything. The little guy was scared as hell; it wasn't his fault his parents were turds. I immediately withdrew my weapon and just told them not to move. I started talking to the boy and told him not to be scared and that he would be fine. I felt bad and really didn't know what else to say to him. I still had a job to do and was not able to leave them unattended until we knew the house was secure.

There's nothing like looking at the scared face of a child and feeling like an asshole. Unfortunately for him, it really was not going to be fine; he ended up going to foster care. All the adults in the house were arrested for possession and distribution of methamphetamines, and his mom was the main dealer. We never knew what happened to this kid after this incident; all adults were sentenced to ten years, and we never saw him again.

Growing up, I had always been boisterous; I was also told many times I didn't need a bullhorn for someone to hear me. We executed a search warrant on a known drug dealer within the town. We knew he was well-armed and did not like law enforcement, as he had threatened to shoot us several times if we came onto his property. After getting the warrant signed and convincing the judge to make it a no-knock warrant, we responded to the residence. Quietly, we lined up outside the front door.

I was the second in line behind the officer with the battering ram, and my job was to locate and detain the suspect as quickly as possible. When all was ready, the first officer hit the door as hard as he could with the ram, which was loud and effective. He hit the door so hard it shattered the doorknob and took the door partially off its hinges. As soon as that door flew open, I was inside and looking for the suspect. The others would detain anybody else we came across.

As I was moving through the living room, I heard a lot of noise coming from the basement and immediately went downstairs. I believed the suspect was attempting to arm himself or destroy evidence, and I was not going to allow either to happen. We did have containment outside of the residence. The local sheriff's department provided deputies to make sure nobody escaped through any windows of the house.

I made my way down the stairs quickly; I do not remember touching the bottom three steps. I saw the suspect and immediately began yelling to show his hands and drop whatever he was holding. I yelled this several times before he turned around to face me. He was attempting to load a rifle but was apparently unsuccessful. As he turned around, I immediately football-tackled him and took him to the ground, knocking the rifle out of his hands. While I was holding him at gunpoint, another officer came downstairs and placed the suspect into handcuffs.

My adrenaline was pumping so hard during this contact that it took me several minutes to calm down. My team leader told me to go outside and cool off and not come back in or talk to the suspect until I had done so. As I was walking outside, I was contacted by one of the deputies standing outside of the house. The basement was above ground and solid brick. The deputy asked if someone inside was using a bullhorn, to which I replied, "No, that was me yelling at the suspect."

The deputy stated, "Damn, son, we could hear you clear as day as if you were standing outside with us... Impressive. Truly impressive." I have always been proud of how loud I can yell, as it does get the attention of many.

When my wife and I were dating early in our relationship, she got to see firsthand how fast we move when we get a SWAT call-out. It was about two o'clock in the morning when my pager went off. The pager was used only for work, so I knew immediately what that meant. Within fifteen minutes, I was up, dressed, and out the door, kissing her goodbye on my way out. I really didn't stop to think about how this looked to her. It was something I was used to; it had become second nature. Anyway, the call-out was a barricaded subject in a neighboring town, and they were asking for our assistance on the call. The normal time for me to get to work was about an hour's drive, but when I got called out, it was much shorter. I made it to the office in about forty-five minutes.

I had a habit of putting on heavy metal music in my vehicle and driving fast to get to where I needed to go. As I got to the office, we completed a quick briefing and headed to the town about ten minutes later; it was only a seven-minute drive to get there. Upon arrival, I grabbed my long gun and found a rooftop where I could see into the building. I was the team sniper at this time, and my spotter was with me. The other five members of the team were preparing to make entry into the residence to get the suspect out. He was holding his wife and daughter hostage.

The local agency wanted him for a warrant for arrest on a domestic violence charge. Unfortunately, he had all the windows covered, so we could not see inside the residence, not even a moving shadow. My spotter and I made our way back down and held cover on the windows from behind a vehicle while the team was preparing to make entry. Right about the time they were getting ready to ram the door, I noticed someone move the window cover from one of the windows, and the window began to open. The local agency chief was using a bullhorn this whole time to try to talk down the suspect and distract him while entry was being made.

As soon as I saw the window opening, I began to yell to the rest of my team since the window was right above them, and we did not know what the suspect was armed with. It's a good thing I am loud, as my team was able to hear me over the chief talking on the bullhorn. They began to back away quickly. As soon as they got out of the way of the window, a pot from a plant came flying out the window, and the window closed again.

This time, the team moved quicker, and entry was made. They were able to get the suspect into custody without anybody being hurt. This was a long night, however, and I did not make it back home until later that afternoon. When I walked into the house, my girlfriend (now wife) was tired and upset. She had been up the whole time worrying about me. I think this was the first time I really thought about how the job affects those around me. I'd never really considered it before; I was focused on the job and lived for it.

This wasn't the only time I scared the hell out of my wife. As we were getting off shift one day, a warrant was issued for another drug house in the town. Now, I would always call my wife after my shift just before I started my journey home. But this day, we had a last-minute SWAT call-out, so I was unable to call her for a few more hours— and even then, I wasn't the one who called her. I had another one of the patrol officers call her for me just to let her know what was going on and the reason she hadn't heard from me yet.

I didn't even think about how she would react to having another officer call her about me. I thought I was doing the right thing just so she knew I was okay and was going to be on duty for a few more hours. When Officer Stanic returned to my location, I could tell something hadn't gone right with the phone call. I asked if he had made contact with her, and he said he did. I asked if everything was okay, and he told me, "Well, I think it is, but I don't think she liked getting a phone call from me, and you may hear about it when you get home tonight."

I instantly knew I should have just called her myself. When I got home, she told me she'd thought something bad had happened when she answered the phone and was told it was Officer Stanic. Again, I learned a valuable lesson that day that many other officers had already learned for themselves: some things you just don't think about until after the fact. I never in my life imagined this would upset her— and again, I thought I was doing the right thing.

As you guessed, we executed a lot of search warrants on several residences throughout the city and into the county. We executed a search warrant six times on one particular house. This place was only two blocks from the police department. We knew the owner, another Jason, was selling meth from the house, but every time we completed a search, we came up empty—except for what was found in his trash each week, which is how we always got the warrants.

Hell hath no fury like a woman scorned; this is a fact. A girl he was dating for a long time had caught him cheating with another female—it was a sex-for-meth type of situation. Apparently, she walked in on him, and it was the last straw. I am pretty sure he knew he'd fucked up—but then again, he also knew we hadn't found anything in the past. This last time was different when we showed up at his house. He was either scared or high and using his own product again, which he was known to do. We knocked on his door at three in the morning and announced, "POLICE! SEARCH WARRANT!"

We could hear movement from the other side of the door. It sounded like someone was moving furniture. Again, we knocked on the door and yelled, "POLICE! SEARCH WARRANT! OPEN THE DOOR NOW!" With the continued movement on the other side of the door, we were pretty sure he was trying to move some type of furniture in front of the door to keep us from coming in. Up to this point, he was always cooperative and would simply open the door with a stupid meth-head smirk on his face and let us in. His smile would expose half the teeth missing from his mouth, and that what was left was black and rotten.

He believed he had found the perfect hiding spot in the past for his meth and we wouldn't discover it. However, this time, we had a leg up: his girlfriend told us exactly where it was. She had him scared, and we were not sure whether she told him she was going to tell us where the drugs were.

We started to kick in the front door because it became obvious that he was not going to open it this time. We could hear him screaming and crying on the other side. When we finally made entry into the house, Jason was curled up in the fetal position on the stairs leading to the second floor of the house. Once we got inside, he was screaming about the devil attacking him and trying to kill him. Right then and there, we knew he was high on meth or something else. He was not worried about us finding anything; he was simply stoned out of his mind.

Every few seconds, he would grin and tell us we weren't going to find anything, no matter how hard we looked. Well, we played the game. We tore the house upside down like we were looking for his drugs and money made from selling. We flipped mattresses on their sides, we took stuff out of the dresser drawers and threw them on the floor, we emptied closets, and we even took everything out of the refrigerator and freezer.

In his madness, he continued to grin and talk shit. I looked at the team and said, "Well, I guess he got us again," and started to walk out the front door. I was the last one heading out the door when I told the rest of the team to hold up for a minute. I turned and went straight out the back door to a porch right outside. The porch was about a foot off the ground. There was a board not screwed down that would be lifted in order to access a drainpipe under the deck that had a screw-on lid.

There was a strong fishing line tied to the inside of the lid. On the other end were small baggies of crystal methamphetamine ready to be sold to the next person; approximately fifty bags were tied together in a line. As I grabbed hold of the meth and started walking into the house, Jason began sobbing uncontrollably. He knew he was caught and was looking at time, as this would be his third felony conviction. Of course, as empathetic as I am (or not), I looked at Jason and stated, "Hell hath no fury, brother. You pissed off the wrong person."

He was then taken into custody, and we never had to execute another search warrant on that residence. Jason was sentenced to twenty-five years to life for his third conviction.

Biker Rally

Every year, the town would host a biker rally. This event was meant to be a POW/MIA commemorative weekend involving a lot of bikers and military personnel. I would walk the casino areas and talk with outlaw bikers. Most common in town were Sons of Silence, Banditos, and Mongols. I don't remember seeing the Outlaws and the Hells Angels. Neither came to town during this weekend, so as not to cause problems.

If you show respect to a biker, you will get it back in return; this was one of the many things I learned about bikers. These guys would walk around rough and gruff, but once you got to know them, they were pretty decent, in a criminal kind of way. I learned about their "code" of how they operate; for example, no child is to ever be harmed during an altercation with another gang. They also hated being called a gang. They would refer to themselves as a club, never admitting their criminal activity behind the scenes.

All-in-all, they policed themselves. If they were unable to take care of their own people causing problems, the president of the gang would step in, and whatever happened after that was hard to say. I took the time every year to attend training from other law enforcement agencies who dealt with these individuals more than we did. I learned a lot from these investigators, like how to talk to the bikers and be upfront with them, which helped in future events. Of course, I did have an early education when I was younger and would hang out at a known biker bar where I grew up. I was never a "hang around," but I would sit and have a great conversation with them. They all knew what I wanted to be and respected that, making sure not to talk too much or give away too much information.

Anyway, this was one of the busiest weekends each year and lasted four days; we would average more than 100,000 people in a one-square-mile town, making it difficult to get patrol cars through the main strip of town, so being on foot was worthwhile. Being a small department, we would bring in police officers from other towns, cities, and counties. There was no way our little department would be able to keep up with all the visitors we would get, especially since it was more than just the bikers. Remember, this was an official POW/MIA commemorative rally, so we would get visitors from all walks of life, including all branches of the military, to show their support and presence.

Since we would be working twelve-to-sixteen-hour shifts, leaving to go home was not an option. When our shift would end, we would sleep in one of the offices at the PD or grab some beds at the fire department (there were never enough firefighters working to fill all the rooms at one time). Even after our shift would end, we would get off work and hang around downtown to watch whatever local entertainment was available during the weekend, whether it was a concert, visiting the beer garden, or just hanging around and looking at all the bikes.

Sometimes, we would hang out with the military folks and drink with them. At the most, we would get about five to six hours of sleep before having to start all over again; this was for those working the day shift. There was too much stuff going on to just go in and fall asleep. Even the graveyard officers would get only a few hours of sleep so they could get up prior to the start of their shift and check stuff out, like the vendor tents, and grab some food before it got too busy.

Needless to say, there was not a lot of sleep to be had from Thursday morning to Sunday night; rest would come when we hit days off. But it was fun. I made several arrests and would have to catch up on paperwork after the weekend ended. This work would usually take a full day to complete, even if I had to go in on my day off.

We hardly ever had any issues with the bikers or military personnel. They were well-behaved for the most part. The worst that would happen was that they may get drunk and a little mouthy—but nothing criminal. The majority of issues were with the locals. They would try to make themselves look tougher than they were; apparently, the whole event was an excuse to be a dumbass.

One of my first cases was dealing with a local who thought he had the right to enter one of the beer gardens without having to pay, simply because he lived in town. He thought it was only fair for locals to get in free to drink, since this event was "invading" their town. From the start, members of the Sons of Silence were playing the security roles on stuff happening outside the casino, so with that in mind, whatever they said was pretty much how it would go.

The local guy who was trying to get into the beer garden was a scrawny character. He stood about five foot six and weighed 150 pounds at the most. The security guy working the garden was about six foot four and weighed well over 250 pounds—not quite a proper match-up for anyone who had a brain. It ended badly for the local guy. He took a swing at the security guy (again, a Sons of Silence member) and was quickly smacked upside the head with a large Mag flashlight.

Guess who lost that fight in a hurry? The local ended up being transported to the hospital by ambulance, and I took over the case. After completing my investigation, I was told to charge the biker for assault, since a weapon was used. This charge was later dropped in the courts. The local, when he returned to town, was also charged with attempted assault and trespassing. He did not win his fight in the courtroom, and he turned out to be one of our biggest problems in the town. He was arrested about seven more times during my career for various other charges. The moral of the story: locals don't have the right to just do whatever they want to do.

During another one of these weekends, we ended up at a bar fight where we had to take several people into custody—again, all local members of the community feeling ten feet tall and bulletproof. One person began resisting the arrest, which turned into a fight in the middle of the street between him, another officer, and myself. He was swinging and kicking as hard as he could to keep from going into handcuffs; ultimately, he lost that fight.

During this altercation, I heard something fly over my head and felt something wet on the side of my face. Then, I heard the clinking of glass. As I looked up, I noticed a beer bottle lying on the ground about five feet from me. As I looked in the direction it came from, I watched a county deputy lift a female off the ground and slam her down face-first on the sidewalk. After she hit the ground, he yelled, "You don't throw fucking beer bottles at cops!" This was when I realized what was on my face and where the glass had come from.

Apparently, the bottle thrower was the wife of the guy I was placing under arrest. She'd decided throwing something at me because I was arresting her husband would be a great idea. Now, she was pissed. I am guessing the one thing she didn't think about was what would happen to her if she completed her task. Due to this being just a fast-and-furious situation, I didn't really got a look at either party right away.

The other officer helping me arrest this guy quickly got him up and moved him toward the jail after we got him in cuffs. The deputy who'd slammed the female onto the ground still had her face- down on the concrete. The most unfortunate part is that I knew both people and had had many good conversations with them prior to this incident. Alcohol does wonders for people when it comes to bravery. It all made the shift go by faster, especially the overtime we had to work because of booking paperwork. The adrenaline got us all going for several more hours.

Bike rallies were known for motorcycle accidents. Even after dealing with so many, you always have one that sticks in your mind (besides the first deadly one, of course). Sometimes, freaky things happen. If you have not seen someone die and come back to life without receiving CPR or first aid, it will be something you will always remember. A group of motorcyclists was coming into town during one of these events. One hit some loose sand that was on the roadway, sending several of them off the road and into a field; of course, none were wearing helmets.

One of the riders was launched off his motorcycle and ended up near a pile of bricks, appearing to have missed them by inches—but thinking back, it was possible he hit the pile and bounced off. Anyway, he had a bad head injury, as could be seen by swelling on the top of his head and the blood around it. I was the first on the scene and immediately made my way to this individual. All the other bikers involved were already up and moving around on their own. I was trying to talk to the injured rider while the ambulance was coming. I was telling him to hang in there; help was coming, and he would be fine.

He had been looking at me the whole time. I wasn't sure if he was really conscious or not, but I was talking to him. It looked like he was in a haze, and I noticed one pupil was bigger than the other. He was moaning a little, as well, but then he stopped, eyes still open. His eyes suddenly went from blue in color to light gray, and he stopped breathing. I tried to find a heartbeat but was unable to locate it anywhere, either on the neck or wrist. I was certain he had died.

I started to yell at him, telling him, "Keep hanging on!" and "Don't die on me." I was anticipating starting CPR but was kind of afraid to since I did not know the extent of his injuries. The paramedics had just arrived and were grabbing their stuff. I continued yelling several times for him to hang in there.

I'm not sure why I was yelling; it was almost like someone talking to a deaf person: if you yell, they might hear you better. I guess I was yelling so that his soul might return to his body. As the medics were walking toward me, his eyes slowly turned blue again, and he took a deep breath in. Scared the hell out of me. I jumped a little. I was not really expecting him to survive.

Shortly after, the medics loaded up the guy and transported him to the hospital. I did learn later that he survived his injuries but had a serious head trauma and may never be the same again—which is unfortunate for him. He was just a weekend biker, not part of any of the gangs we got in town.

While learning all I could about biker gangs, I discovered what certain patches on their jackets or vests meant, and even what it means when a badge is upside down. I enjoyed learning what I could to improve my knowledge. However, I also put it to use just to fuck with these guys every now and then.

While talking to one member of the Sons of Silence, I noticed the "M" patches on the upper part of his jacket, so I thought I would see what he would say about them if asked. He told me it was because he liked money and his mother a lot. He displayed them for his mom. Of course, I called bullshit. As he was trying to convince me of what the M stood for, I said, "So, money, meth, murder, and mayhem have nothing to do with your wearing those patches."

He then became agitated and said, "If you knew what they stood for, why even ask me?" I said, "Just wanted to see what you would say or admit to." As he turned to walk away, he said, "These fucking cops think they are so funny. Fucking assholes." It was a learning experience for me to see what they will admit to; they do give the dumbest answers ever when asked.

The final weekend of working these biker events was in 2006—firstly, because I was planning on going to a larger department; and secondly, because the city did not want to host another year and was allowing another town to take on the rally. This was the year when the Banditos motorcycle club made it their national mandatory run, meaning there were going to be members from all over the world hanging around town. On the first day of the rally, I noticed several members from the Washington chapter ride into town; they were the first batch making their way in.

I decided to take this opportunity to introduce myself and let them know the information I was privy to and what was to be expected. This was a trick I learned from one of the trainings I attended, taught by the Colorado Bureau of Investigations. All the members were parked in front of one of the bars in town, and I saw the president of the chapter sitting outside of the establishment. I pulled my car over and got out, making contact with him.

He stood up and watched me walk over to him. I introduced myself, shaking his hand, and let him know I knew this was a mandatory run for all Banditos. I advised him, since he was the first president I'd seen come in, that it was expected they police themselves and that he would be responsible for any issues that came about from this run. He would be held solely accountable for any trouble any of his members caused over the weekend. He took a step back and looked me up and down. His face said he did not enjoy this initial introduction.

After a few seconds, though, he began to smile. He shook my hand again and said, "I can respect that. I don't need or want any trouble to happen while we're here, and I know you all will be watching us." At that moment, I was able to breathe again. I hadn't known what to expect. For the next hour and a half, we sat on a bench in front of the bar and had some great conversation. There was a mutual respect between us. This was a great meeting to have.

As the weekend began and things started to kick off, more and more riders came into town. On the second day of the rally, things were at full throttle, and there were hundreds of Banditos in town, including prospects for the club. While walking the strip where the event was happening, we passed by one of the casinos where a couple of prospects were sitting. As I looked over at them—and I was watching everyone—one of the prospects for the Banditos stood up from his bench and began talking shit to my partner and me.

He started off with, "What the fuck are you pigs looking at? You want trouble? I have no problems with that. Or you can keep walking like the pussies I know you are." I walked straight up to this prospect. I noticed the president I met the day prior sitting behind him, not really paying attention. I didn't say anything to the prospect. Instead, I looked around the prospect and past him, where I made eye contact with the president of the Washington chapter.

As I made eye contact, I asked the president, "Do I take care of this problem, or do you?" He immediately stood up and started yelling at the prospect to "sit the fuck down and shut the fuck up." He told the prospect he was not to speak or even look my direction moving forward, or he would find himself in a world of pain. The prospect, obviously pissed off, turned away from me, mumbling under his breath, and sat back down. Nothing more was said from that moment on, and no further issues happened with them for the rest of the weekend.

Although no issues came about from the Banditos, we did have a local group of idiots who decided they wanted to be members of the Booze Fighters, another biker gang well-known throughout the state and many other places. Apparently, they thought they needed to look badass in front of all the other bikers in town and started talking shit to us officers walking the area. It didn't matter which officer; they were talking shit to all of us.

These moronic dumbasses were all locals and worked for the city, in the road and water department. Knowing them, I decided to make contact and let them know if they did not stop, we were going to make a fool of all members and arrest them all. I added insult to injury as I advised that not only would they be arrested and booked into jail for the weekend, but I would also take their colors and place them into evidence so they could not get them back until after court. Without their colors, nobody would care who they were, and they would just be known as a bunch of wannabes pretending to be bad. They would lose their chapter from the club hosting them.

This shut them down pretty quickly, especially after the chief, deputy chief, and city manager backed me up on their little complaint they made that I was being unprofessional and mean to them. Some people just don't get it right away; but they learn over time.

Don't get me wrong here. We had our share of getting into trouble during these events, as well. My partner and I would run errands for the Marines at the rally, mainly because my partner was a Marine at one time and would do anything for them. In return, we both would get cases of Meals Ready to Eat, or MREs, at no charge. We kept stocked up for several years doing this.

One time, we had a young officer who had asked one of the female Marines out on a date. I'm not sure what she told him, but apparently, she turned him down pretty hard and hurt his feelings. As the day went on, she got to feeling bad about it. So, to make up, she was going to allow him to Taser her one time, which he was more than willing to do. The problem is, when one Marine gets tased, the rest take it as a challenge, thinking they can last longer. We wound up tasing approximately thirty Marines that day, including a retired Marine who happened to show up while the others were taking a ride of lightning, thinking we were out of sight of the public. However, we were not; our deputy chief saw what was going on and was not happy or amused. He did wait until we were done.

While leaving the area, he contacted my partner and me and chewed our asses for about twenty minutes. His final word was, "You all will stay away from the Marines for the rest of the weekend. Let the other officer know if I catch any of you around them for anything other than a call for service, all involved will be suspended immediately for three days without pay. We passed this information on to the rest of the team. We found it amusing that he waited until we were all done with the tasing to talk to us instead of contacting us right away and stopping what we were doing. It makes me wonder what he really thought about the situation.

Biker weekend, or the POW/MIA rally, was something we looked forward to every year. It wore us out, but all in all, it was busy and exciting, we never knew what was going to happen, good or bad. For the most part, it was simply a blast; there wasn't an officer who did not want to work the weekend, and there was plenty of overtime paid out.

Deaths and Suicides

There were good days, great days, and bad days. Good days were having the ability to talk to citizens and visitors in the town. I would sit and have coffee with the locals and maybe have a meal. It was nice when I was able to do this without being interrupted by a call for service, and I got to learn a lot about the history of families and the town. It was interesting to learn how much history was within this little place, especially the family histories and how many generations have actually been part of the community. Then there were those bad days, dealing with deaths.

Suicides were plenty in this small town, whether intentional or not. By intentional, I mean those intending to kill themselves, whether by overdose, hanging, or weapon. Unintentional were those who were only threatening to kill themselves, and in the process of making that threat to their significant other, the gun they were holding went off, causing them to shoot themselves in the head. This happened only twice, and there was one overdose that went awry. Sometimes, these situations get strange.

We responded to a call in the middle of town for a man threatening to shoot himself in the head while standing in the street. During his rantings, we found out his wife had cheated on him. Instead of leaving her, he wanted her to know just how much he was hurt by her. He was saying that if he killed himself, it would "fuck her up enough to never want another man."

We tried hard to get him to put down the gun—a .44 magnum handgun, a hand cannon—but he just kept yelling, "That bitch needs to learn a lesson." His wife was an employee in one of the casinos and heard the ruckus going on. It was happening right in front of her job. As soon as she walked out the front doors, he turned to face her and yelled, "Think of another man while you are fucking them now, bitch!" He then pulled the trigger.

Now, I have heard this type of weapon will make someone's head explode, but I was not sure I believed that until I actually saw the carnage. There was not much left. Once we all realized what had actually happened and the screaming stopped from the people watching it, we were all kind of amazed he'd actually shot himself.

I'm not sure whether she learned the lesson or not, but it did shake her up quite a bit in the moment. I am sure any citizen who watched the side of someone's head explode like a watermelon with a stick of dynamite in it would be shaken up, though. Unfortunately for him, it didn't affect her the way he was hoping for; she moved in with her boyfriend the next day.

While driving to work on Halloween morning, I was contacted by Sgt. Riker and asked to hurry and grab my car and come to his location. So, I rushed to the department, swapped all my gear over to my patrol car, and responded to the call. Sgt. Riker was working on a case where a person had committed suicide by hanging. When I arrived on the scene, Sgt. Riker told me he'd seen the victim hanging while patrolling the area—but he hadn't thought it was real, considering the time of year, so he'd continued to drive around some more. He just kept driving around the block because something didn't seem right. He stopped to take a closer look and realized the body was real. So, he figured he'd better do something about it.

During the investigation, it was determined the victim had struggled with a serious drug and gambling problem. Being broke, he wasn't able to eat, and he'd had to have his dog put down the week before. Being in a depressed state, he hanged himself from a tree in his front yard using his dog's leash. Apparently, Halloween seemed like the right day to do it.

When I arrived on the scene, Sgt. Riker had already placed a sheet over the body to keep anybody from seeing it, especially kids who were about to leave their homes and head to school. The problem was that the coroner could not get to our location for several hours, as they were dealing with other deaths within the county. I told my sergeant we should be able to leave him up with the sheet covering him, since it was Halloween.

It would not have been noticed as easily, and the coroner could get to the location whenever they had time. He found the comment funny, and my coworkers agreed with me. I still had to stay on scene until the coroner arrived about six hours later. Being in a town where drugs (specifically, methamphetamines) were plenty, overdoses were bound to happen—some intentional, and some not so much.

Then, there was the hard way to kill oneself. One guy tried to do it by driving head-on into the side of a mountain. He was not successful. He only crippled himself for a while, breaking both of his legs. We had received a call of a suicidal party driving recklessly around town and located him. He was in a pickup truck and going too fast, running stop signs, and even driving on the wrong side of the road at times.

When we got behind him, he decided to run from us, and so the vehicle chase was on. Back then, we were allowed to chase cars. During the pursuit down a winding dirt road, we followed him for approximately a mile and a half—until we saw him nearing a sharp curve in the road with a rocky ridge on one side and a cliff on the other. As he approached the curve, he turned toward the rock side and went straight into the side of the mountain at approximately sixty miles per hour. Again, this did nothing more than break both his legs. After being transported to the hospital, he was able to go home within a few hours.

I think one of the worst suicides I responded to was a previous dispatcher we had at the department, Linda. Of course, anytime someone you know kills themselves, it can shake you up. We had responded several weeks prior to a domestic violence dispute between Linda and her significant other. Following the investigation, Linda's significant other was arrested, and a court order was put in place to keep her away from Linda and the house.

On top of that, Linda had been fired from the department due to being intoxicated at the start of her shift. When the option was provided for her to get counseling and attend Alcoholics Anonymous on the department's dime, she told Chief Johnson, "Go fuck yourself." Between being fired and not being able to see her significant other, Linda couldn't handle it any longer and decided to take her own life with a .410 shotgun under the chin.

Having a forensic background, Linda thought covering herself with a heavy blanket would ensure there was not such a big mess. However, the blanket did nothing to contain the blast and head and brain matter. Upon our arrival at the scene, we could smell the blood and gunpowder in the air, and the burnt hair and skin. The smell is hard to describe and also unforgettable.

I remember seeing her lying on her back on the bed and the shotgun lying on the floor by her feet, where it fell after the shot. The sight and the smell in the room were the kind that would stick with a person no matter how hard they might try to forget it. The blanket used to cover everything was stuck to the ceiling and could be heard slowly starting to fall. It made a sucking sound, and when it fell, brains and chunks of skull went everywhere.

We'd included the new recruit we had in training. Some people can handle this job, and some can't; this is a good way to tell. In this case, the recruit turned green and ran out of the house. When I went to check on him later, he handed me his badge and gun and said he quit and could not handle a scene like that. Linda's being someone known to the department for a long time, and a previous coworker, affected several of us at the department—some more than others, and some in more noticeable ways.

Linda was the third person I had worked with in the police field who had committed suicide. Her death happened not long after the homicide of a brother at the sheriff's department. The first suicide I knew of was a previous deputy who worked at the sheriff's department, who took his own life while his wife and daughter were in the bedroom with him. The second was the sergeant who'd been in charge of placing Ken at the arson scene, a decision which had resulted in Ken's murder.

The sheriff at the time solely blamed this sergeant for Ken's death. The sergeant took his own life in his living room by placing a .357 Magnum handgun to his chest in front of a plate glass window. The blast of the weapon blew the sergeant backward and through the glass. His family blamed the department and allowed no law enforcement at his funeral. After losing four people in a four-year period, it was starting to get to me, but I hid it very well. I just continued to get angrier and saltier as time went on.

The unintentional suicides came through the use of auto-erotic asphyxiation, kids daring each other to do something stupid, or overdosing on drugs like meth and heroin. These deaths were just as bad as any of the deaths we dealt with, but the kids were the worst; their bad decisions caused them to die. Their deaths would make you think about the safety of your own children and worry about their decisions.

We responded to a heroin overdose where a teenager had taken too much on his first try. We were told he had previously experimented with shrooms, acid, and some meth before deciding to try heroin. He was told how much to use by the dealer he got it from. This information came from his girlfriend, who had been with this young man when he died.

He injected the amount the dealer told him to and passed out. His girlfriend had only smoked some weed. When she woke up, he was not breathing, and his lips were blue. By the time we got to the scene, he was already gone. It was apparent he had been dead for several hours. Even so, as was protocol, we called the ambulance, and the medics took care of the rest.

At the time of this incident, I was a married man with a daughter going into her teenage years. The death of the young man was hitting too close to home for me. I knew there were plenty of other things to worry about as she got older, and this was just one more thing. These kinds of calls make it difficult not to take the job home and not to think of how you can make sure the same thing does not happen to your own. Unfortunately, you realize you cannot watch them 100 percent of the time, and you hope, just hope, they make the right choices as they get older. All you can do is just hug them when you get home and tell them how much you love them. They may not understand why you hug them so tight, and your spouse probably wonders the same. Some stories, you do not take home. You protect your spouse and your children from the disturbing things you deal with daily.

Adult deaths are something you get used to seeing after a while, and with a twisted sense of humor one starts to develop after working this job. The humor was one way we coped with seeing death regularly. We dealt with several adult overdoses from drugs or alcohol, along with a couple of deaths caused by auto-erotic asphyxiation that occurred while the victims were alone. We found a man hanging in his closet by a belt he had wrapped around the closet rack, his cock in hand. It was apparent he had passed out and choked to death while jerking off. Sad as it was, it did happen.

The majority of our deaths in the city were from natural causes due to health issues or alcoholism. We responded to a call one night for an older gentleman who had apparently woken up in the mood for sex during the night. He'd rolled over and woken up his wife, telling her he wanted sex. She told him she was not in the mood and to go take care of it himself. When he rolled back over, he apparently had a heart attack and died.

We felt bad for the wife because she felt responsible. This is the part of the job that requires one to have empathy and not say anything stupid or sarcastic, causing further trauma. On the other hand, it is very difficult to be serious and show empathy when the guy is lying there with a full-on erection that lasted even after the body was taken to the coroner's office. We were guessing he took a little blue pill. He was placed in the body bag while being fully erect, making the body bag look like a tent. We were able to keep a straight face and remain professional. However, once we cleared the scene, we let loose with the jokes.

Another call we responded to was a very heavy gentleman who drank himself to death. We were dispatched to conduct a welfare check because his family had not heard from him in several days. When we arrived at the house, I felt something was not right. Know one thing: if you smell a dead body that has been in the heat for several days, it will never be forgotten. You will be able to recognize that smell anywhere, at any scene, after smelling it once.

When I approached the front door, I could immediately smell death coming through the door. The house was completely shut off, with the curtains closed and all doors closed and locked. Not being able to find a way in, we had to kick the front door open. As soon as we did, the putrid smell hit us in the face, a combination of rotting corpse and vodka. When we made entry, the male was sprawled across the couch. His underside was all black, and the flies were swarming.

This incident happened in the middle of summer when the temperatures were hitting the mid to upper nineties. Having no air conditioning, the victim was baking inside the house. As we went and checked for a pulse, just to make sure, we noticed seven empty one-gallon bottles of vodka lying on the floor next to the couch. The detective was working that day, for what that was worth, and came to the scene just in case there were suspicious circumstances floating about, anything hinting at foul play. The only things the detective found floating were the individuals' eyelids. They were moving, but not in a waking-up kind of way. Still, the detective started yelling that the individual was alive and that we needed to start resuscitating him.

I advised this detective there were plenty of signs to show the man was deceased, and the movement under his eyelids was not him trying to wake up. I told the detective to take a look around and notice all the flies. The detective began to argue with me, so I walked him back to the body and opened the man's eyelids. It was not flickering eyeballs the detective had seen underneath; it was maggots moving around.

As much as I enjoyed showing the detective how much of an idiot he was, it gave me more pleasure to watch the detective run out the door to vomit, especially because we were told time and again how tough they were and how much they could handle. This detective found out how much he could *not* handle.

Anyway, we had to get the body out of the house, and this was a very big man who weighed well over four hundred pounds. We called the firefighters over for help, and as we were talking, they decided it would be best to place the man onto a backboard and drag him out of the house using a four-wheeler, which we did in the middle of the day, with everyone and their dog watching. It's not something anybody really wants to have to do; but sometimes, we have to improvise and make things work to our advantage.

Not everyone considers someone who commits suicide a victim. Usually, the rest of the family and friends are the victims of someone who kills themselves. However, there are times when someone who commits suicide is truly

136

a victim of the way they were raised and society's expectations of them. Jarod was one of these cases. I got to know Jarod when he was in middle school.

There were days when I would have coffee with some of the bus drivers for the school district, and Jarod would come by the bus barn during his lunch or right after school because he wanted to learn to be a mechanic. The supervisor, Dale, and one of the drivers, Billy, were mechanics on the buses, and Jarod would go in and learn from these two. He did little odd jobs throughout the bus barn, such as sweeping the floor and picking up tools left lying around, making sure to put them where they belonged.

When it was just Dale, Billy, and me at the barn, Jarod would talk to us about his personal issues at home. He really wanted to be a good kid. However, his dad was in prison for multiple different crimes, so he was raised by his mother, who would talk shit about Jarod every time we saw her. She was one of the bus drivers. She would tell us how Jarod wouldn't listen at home and was hanging out with the wrong crowd, and that she fully expected him to end up in prison just like his father.

We would constantly tell her Jarod was a good kid and wanted to do right. He was always respectful to us when he was in the shop, to which she would reply, "Just wait and see. He will end up in prison." Jarod would tell us she would constantly say these things to him as well. It was hard to be professional and nice when she was around. It got to the point where she would leave as soon as I walked into the bus barn because I would tell her she needed to stop saying these things to Jarod. She would just tell me to mind my own business, and she would raise him how she wanted.

Well, as Jarod got older, into his late teens, he started to get into trouble. I guess when it is expected of you, you might as well become the criminal mom is sure you will be. He was mostly getting arrested for domestic violence against his girlfriend. I had to pepper-spray him once while trying to take him into custody. He had no idea I was even at the scene of the arrest. Jarod later told me if he had known I was one of the officers there to arrest him, he would not have fought back. We had a mutual respect for one another. Jarod and his family lived in the county, about two miles outside of town.

While monitoring the county deputies' radio traffic, I heard the call come in that Jarod had possibly killed himself after he and his mom got into a heated argument. I recognized the address that was aired and decided to respond, as I had known Jarod for approximately ten years by then. When I arrived on the scene, a deputy was already talking to Jarod's mom, and I overheard her say nonchalantly, "Yeah, he's under the car. He shot himself in the head. We had an argument, and I told him the best thing he could do was just kill himself and do everyone else a favor."

She continued, "So, he grabbed his gun and crawled under the car and shot himself. Good riddance is all I can say." When I heard this, I went to the car and looked underneath, and there was Jarod, a gun still in hand and a bullet wound to the side of his head. Jarod was no longer with us, and I was livid. I spun around and asked his mom, "What the fuck is wrong with you? You have to be the biggest piece of shit on this planet, and if there was a way to hold you accountable and charge you with his death, you can damn well bet I would."

She then just flipped me the bird and walked back inside. To this day, I still don't have the words to explain how pissed off I was. This was one of those cases where being left alone was all you wanted. It was hard to fight back the tears over such a senseless death; but then again, no matter how hard you try, you just can't save them all.

We didn't just respond to suicides on calls and in town. If you remember, I also lost friends and colleagues to suicide. There was the officer who killed himself in front of his family, and there was the officer who killed himself because he felt responsible for Ken's death at the arson house—according to his family, he had become seriously depressed and wasn't himself toward the end but wouldn't seek help—and there was Linda. After Linda, one more took his own life. He was a state trooper. I met John for the first time when he gave me a careless driving ticket. As I was heading to work one morning, I hit black ice on the roadway and spun into another vehicle. John was already on the scene at another accident and apparently was not happy he had been called out for this accident. Since he was there and had watched my accident, he told me I couldn't leave until after I got my summons for causing it.

Keep in mind there was very minor damage to both vehicles and no injuries. The other driver was a nurse heading to work, and we both just wanted to get going. Anyway, a couple of years later, I saw John again at my department writing up someone for driving under the influence. While he was there, we started talking about that accident. He chuckled a little and told me, "You should have just gone to court. I was in a bad mood that morning, and after giving you the ticket, you knew I wasn't going to appear if you fought it."

I called him an asshole and told him how I wished I would have known then what I knew now. We became friends after that and would meet up once in a while for breakfast and to shoot the shit. He was older than me and was proud when he finally got married for the first time. He admitted he was too tied up with work to consider dating or getting married, but this happened out of the blue for him, and he was happy.

A year later, he and his wife got into an argument, and he punched her in the face. It sounded like he knew he was in trouble after that, and his career was on the line. If he was charged with domestic violence, he would lose his job and never be able to work again in law enforcement. He took off from the house in his state patrol car. Nobody really knows why he was aimlessly driving around.

After the local department left his house from responding to his wife's reporting of the assault, they came across John and tried to pull him over. He led them on a short pursuit and then pulled into a church parking lot, and when the local officers were approaching his vehicle, he shot himself in the head with his duty gun. To this day, it angers me that he committed such a cowardly act in front of officers in a town where he lived and knew everyone—but he wasn't the only one and probably won't be the last when it comes to those taking their own life for their fellow officers to find.

Dealing with deaths and suicides is not an easy task, and you never really get used to it. You just sort of grown numb to it. The hardest part about dealing with these calls was making the notifications to the families, if they did not know already. Having to knock on somebody's door to tell them their son, daughter, brother, sister, or significant other had passed away puts a knot in your stomach you never get used to feeling. I did not like notifying the deceased's loved ones, but I was glad to be there to help them through their grief in whatever way I was able.

That is not the worst or hardest thing one can do when it comes to responding to a death call. Holding the hand of someone while they are dying and trying to convince them they'll be okay to keep them calm possibly ranks at the top for worst calls. As I responded to a traffic accident, I noticed the vehicle was flipped upside down, lying on top of a very large boulder. I ran to the driver's side of the vehicle. The driver was still alive. He was conscious and breathing heavily.

With tears in his eyes, he continuously asked me to tell his family he loved them and that he was sorry. Since I did not have the tools to cut him out of the vehicle, all I could do was sit with him and tell him he was going to be okay and that the fire department was on the way. Unfortunately, the fire department was on another call outside of town and was going to be at least fifteen minutes out.

The injuries to the driver appeared to be fatal; he was losing a lot of blood fast. I looked for where the blood was coming from to try and stop it but couldn't find the wound. I had about four inches of opening between the top of the door frame to the roof of the vehicle, not much to work with. Forcing him out of the vehicle was not something I was trained to do. Aside from that issue, I had no one to help me, since my partner was transporting a prisoner to the jail twenty-five miles away.

All I could do was sit with the driver and try to comfort him. After what seemed like forever but was, in reality, only about two to three minutes after my arrival, he started to slip in and out of consciousness. I was able to reach his neck to check his pulse. I could reach his wrist and check his pulse there, as well. I noticed it was getting weaker quickly, and the blood continued to fall onto the roof and the ground outside the car, soaking into my pants.

Sometimes, being covered in blood has to be ignored. I was not about to leave him alone because my pants were getting soaked. About ten minutes in, I could hear the sirens of the fire truck and ambulance in the distance and knew they were getting closer. I just kept saying, "Hold on, rescue is coming. They will get you out. Just stay awake for me." Just before fire personnel got to my location, the driver lost consciousness for the final time, and I was unable to wake him. I kept yelling, "Hang in there, buddy! They are almost here! Don't die on me now!" However, I was unable to find a pulse and knew I had lost him. The driver had died.

Hands and pants covered in blood, I had to gather my wits and meet the fire and rescue team to advise. After they were able to get his body out of the car, it was learned he would not have survived anyway, as the dashboard had severed his right leg from just above the knee. He would not have made it, no matter what. I got cleaned up and changed my uniform. Then, I decided I would notify his family and relay his message to them.

Domestic Violence Calls

For a small town of one square mile, we had a hell of a lot of domestic violence calls. Most were due to gambling and drinking issues of one or both of the parties involved. Of course, I suppose when there is nothing better to do than drink and gamble, arguments are bound to happen between couples. And the drunker they get, the more violent the fight becomes.

About nine out of ten times, one of them went to jail because the fighting wouldn't end. They would just keep going until someone was struck, which tied our hands at that point, and someone would have to be arrested. Early on in my career, we would have the option to arrest someone or use these opportunities to educate younger couples. Those with more experience than me taught me to expect the following: If they were young and fighting, it was probably because of money, and things would get out of hand. There would be one person in the relationship who would be spending money at the casinos or drinking all night, and the other would get pissed because they were behind on bills and about to lose their electricity or home.

We thought this kind of scenario was a great opportunity to educate these young couples on how to deal with such issues in a way that didn't involve getting violent with each other. Most of the time, it worked, and there would be no more responses to these houses. Family counseling was part of the job, and we had to learn different methods, especially if arresting one of the parties would mean they would have to come up with money to bail out and to cover court costs. We felt if they were having money problems to begin with, then arresting them was not going to make their problems any better.

However, being in such a small town, we would also arrest the same people over and over again for domestic violence. Most were the men who would go to jail after assaulting their wife/partner, and then the following day, they would be back in their homes having made up and said they were sorry. This is a pattern that is seen often, by many officers.

After responding to these assaults multiple times in the same house over a long period, I have to admit I would have no sympathy for the victim and couldn't even show empathy. We did have one couple we responded to about seven times in one month. He would strike her in places that didn't show bruises in public, and she would call us each time it happened. Of course, he was never at the house when we arrived, so we would have to figure out which bar he was at, and he would resist and try to fight back while we were there arresting him.

One time, she had to be transported to the hospital and placed into intensive care for six weeks, which was the last straw. She was finally able to leave him. Due to the extent of the injuries he had caused, he was not allowed to see her while she was hospitalized, per a court order—and the nurses made sure it was enforced. You know, after so many times of dealing with the same people, you just lose compassion. I guess that could be the case for a lot of calls that have the same victims time and again.

Domestic violence calls are dangerous to respond to, as we never know what we are truly getting ready to come into. Sometimes, the victim would attack us for arresting their significant other. Sometimes, the suspect would be armed, and we would have no idea.

I can recall one domestic violence call I was dispatched to that made me think I wouldn't make it through alive. There is a feeling you get on certain calls, about things easily going wrong or about to go wrong, and that it could result in someone not surviving the incident. This is never a good feeling, and it is one all first responders get. The call was a physical domestic dispute for a husband who had a firearm and had taken off into a field surrounding the house. The problem was that I didn't know he was armed until I was approaching the residence on foot, and dispatch aired it about the time I spotted the victim. The victim was very upset, and all she could do was say, "He's going to kill us both!"

Once I was able to get her to calm down enough to talk to me, she advised me that, during their argument, he pushed past her and grabbed a pistol he kept in their closet. She told me he then pointed the gun at himself and threatened to shoot himself in the head. When he heard my siren, he pointed the gun at her and told her he would kill her if he was found, along with anybody who tried to arrest him.

The victim had no idea where he had gone or the direction he took when he traveled into the field surrounding their house; she just knew he was armed with a handgun she watched him load prior to threatening her. While talking to her, the only cover I had was between the house and their car. She repeatedly screamed, "Don't leave me. He'll come back and kill me!"

The whole time, while en route and after making contact with the victim, I had a partner who was on a traffic stop and did not turn his handheld radio on to hear the dispatcher send us the call. Dispatch and I tried numerous times to get my partner on the radio to tell him I was responding. Due to the situation, I went ahead and continued to the scene; we are trained not to allow someone to be killed, and I was not about to just stand back and watch this happen while my partner was fucking around on a traffic stop.

During my contact with the victim, I heard my partner call for a clearance on his driver and just started rambling off information. Once he was done talking, dispatch and I again started calling him on the radio to get him to end the stop and respond. Again, we received no answer or response from him. It was at this point I started to get that sick sense that this was not going to end well. I had a victim frantic about me walking away to look for the suspect and a partner with his head so far up his own ass he had no idea what the hell was happening—except for that he had to finish that damn traffic stop.

I continued to stay with the victim to get what information I could and air that information to whoever had a radio and could respond. I was surrounded by 360 degrees of open field, with very little cover and no idea of where the suspect went. The feeling of a possible bad ending was getting even stronger. Trying to maintain a 360-degree view, looking for the suspect, and calming the hysterical victim (who kept trying to get closer to me) so I could understand what she was saying, I continued calling for cover. I was doing my best to keep her next to the house where she at least had some type of cover from the suspect.

After several minutes of no response from my coworker (or anybody), I decided just to stand by and wait, hoping the suspect wasn't going to come out of the bushes or from wherever he was hiding and start shooting. The victim and I were completely exposed to the suspect. I was advised by dispatch that there was a record of the suspect being aggressive toward cops, and now he had a gun. The feeling continued to grow.

At one point, I knew I wasn't going to make it home that night. I kept talking to the victim while doing my best to watch for the suspect—but we can't do all that at once, and something usually goes wrong. I couldn't go look for the suspect because the victim kept trying to follow me; and I had no idea where to look, anyway. Being only one person, I had no choice but to stay where I was.

I also couldn't leave the victim in case the suspect came back and tried to make good on his threat. I had fallen into the mindset that this could very well be my last call, but I would do it, making sure the victim survived. It seemed to me that it was taking forever to get somebody to respond to my calls for a cover officer. Time was standing still. However, it only ended up being about ten minutes of being there by myself when I heard sirens and screeching tires heading toward me. I was thinking, it's about fucking time he heard the radio. I hadn't heard my partner say anything on the radio, but I figured that could have been due to tunnel vision while dealing with the situation.

Unbeknownst to me, this was not my coworker coming to cover me; this was actually a division of gaming agent working in the town at the casinos. He was from another agency whose primary job was dealing with gambling crimes and issues, not responding to calls of this nature. I guess it didn't matter who was coming; cover was on the way, and my tension and fear eased up a little. Still, the feeling was there. I could now focus on keeping the victim calm while having my back watched at the same time. Once Agent Thompson arrived, I instructed the victim to stay where she was. Agent Thompson and I then started the search for the suspect. He went around one side of the house, and I went around the other.

We had worked together for several years; both had tactical training and understood how to make sure to identify each other when we met around the back, so neither one of us shot the other. After several minutes, we were able to find the suspect. He was trying to hide in a little crawl space under the house in a dark corner. As soon as we saw him, we immediately started giving him commands to drop the weapon and show his hands. This cowardly fuck immediately began crying, begging us not to shoot him.

He quickly threw the pistol on the ground and raised his hands. After we got him into custody, I picked up the gun and found out he had no live rounds in the weapon. The stupid shit damn near got his ass shot for carrying a pistol with blanks in the cylinder. When we got him into custody and walked him around to the front of the house, I could hear my partner, Officer Olivera, finally responding, screaming through town in the middle of the night, lights and sirens blaring after I'd already advised the suspect was in custody.

As he arrived on the scene, he said, "When did this call come out? I never heard anything on the radio." Boy, did I verbally rip into him! I told him if he had his radio turned on, he would have heard the call and me yelling for cover while he was on some dumbass traffic stop. I asked Olivera if he at least gave the driver a ticket, and that was the reason it took so long. He told me he gave the driver a verbal warning, and they began talking about Hawaii. I was so fucking pissed at this point that I actually lunged for him wanting to just kick the shit out of this idiot I was working with.

Luckily, Agent Thompson saw this coming and grabbed hold of me before I could do something stupid. Not only was Agent Thompson a good cover, but he was also a good friend. Once he calmed me down and advised Olivera to talk to the victim and get the rest of the story, Agent Thompson and I left to transport the suspect. It took a while, but I did calm down after a bit. I just wouldn't talk to my partner for the rest of the shift unless I really had to.

In my short time in this career, I had heard about officers writing a letter to their loved ones and keeping it in their locker or someplace safe. These letters told their family how much they loved them and what the officer's wishes would be moving forward. The letters usually weren't read unless the officer was killed in the line of duty. Following this call, I determined a letter may be a good idea, although I'd made it out alive up to this point. One just never knows what could happen in the future. Following this call, I sat down and wrote a letter to my parents, telling them how much I loved them and what I wanted done if something did happen to me. This letter was taped inside my work locker, only to be found if I was killed.

After I got married, I wrote another to my wife. Then, when my youngest was born, I wrote another to both my kids. I had three letters written that I kept taped safely in my locker, only to be opened if something happened to me. I kept these letters from this department and later took them with me to the next. The letters were destroyed the day I retired from law enforcement, as they were no longer needed.

Anyway, back to the call and the non-responding partner I worked with, here is the topper to the whole incident: Several days later, my sergeant pulled me aside and verbally reprimanded me for responding to the call alone. He told me Olivera had said I was mean to him and tried to strike him during the call for no reason. After I told him about Olivera not responding to the radio, even to dispatch, about the call, he told me nothing was going to happen to Olivera.

It didn't matter whether he could hear the radio or not. I should not have responded to that call alone, no matter how much danger the victim may have been in. I always thought our job was to respond no matter what and protect those who were in danger; but apparently, that was not what my coworker or sergeant thought. Let's just say Olivera and I never got along after this; I was switched to a different team to get away from him.

However, payback was easy with Olivera. Within a year following the incident, he was promoted to sergeant. Yes, I know. How does someone as stupid as him get promoted to sergeant? Well, in a small agency, you kiss enough ass, and eventually, you get what you want: a promotion where you can now try to boss people around and tell them what to do.

Unfortunately for him, I didn't play that game, and he wasn't my sergeant. Anyway, I was asked to cover a shift for one of the officers on his team due to a family situation, which I had no problem with. Well, Sgt. Olivera had made a traffic stop, and it turned out to be a very drunk individual driving the vehicle. After I arrived as a cover officer at the traffic stop, Olivera performed roadside maneuvers on the driver.

During roadsides, the driver shit his pants while doing the walk-and-turn. Sgt. Olivera, not wanting to transport the driver now, advised I was to transport the driver to the jail because he didn't want this stinky individual in his patrol car. There were only two of us on duty, and one of us had a bad attitude and did not like the other. I told him this was not going to happen, and since this was his traffic stop and his report, he needed to transport the driver himself.

You know— the "you catch 'em, you clean 'em" mentality. He tried his best to order me to transport the driver, and again, I told him, "Yeah, I don't think so." He even threatened to have me written up for insubordination. The problem was this was not an order that would be enforceable by the chief. Even the chief knew if you made the stop, you transported the arrestee, even if they had shit themselves. So, with that, I got in my car and drove away.

The suspect was in custody, and so drunk he couldn't even stand on his own. I left Sgt. Olivera with his driver, so he had to transport this stinky individual himself. Knowing the stench he was going to have to smell for an hour-long ride in the car was payback enough. The better part of this call: It was in the middle of winter, and Sgt. Olivera hated the cold, so I knew he would be transporting with the windows up and the heat blasting. Believe me, this dude stunk, and the possible reprimand was well worth it!

By the time this happened, I was getting crustier and didn't much care who I pissed off. I certainly wasn't going to put up with anybody's shit or a sergeant who thought he could tell people to do things he was not willing to do himself. Sgt. Olivera was not the only sergeant I didn't care for, and I didn't have any qualms about letting them know how I felt. We did have another sergeant with the same mentality of "do as I say, not as I do": Sgt. Melbourne.

We were expected to do whatever we were told to do that he didn't want to do himself, because he was a supervisor. Melbourne was not my direct sergeant, either; he was a detective sergeant. My sergeant backed me every time I would tell Sgt. Melbourne to do the job himself, especially if there was something needing to be done from an investigation he was working on. It was no secret we did not like or even respect each other. I really needed nobody else's approval when it came to doing my job, how I felt about others, or how I acted and thought.

For a small department, we went through several sergeants in the time I was there. Some thought they were pretty special and earned no respect from anybody within the department, and others were pretty damn good. The good did outweigh the bad for the most part. Fortunately, I outlasted most of them at the department, so I would watch many come and go and happily work my patrol shifts. Honestly, it is hard to believe I wasn't fired for not following their orders. Somehow, I skated through with my insubordination and bad attitude. Crazy how that shit works.

I did have a lot of great days working with this department, and within the first year, I knew I would be doing this for as long as I could. I found a job I truly enjoyed and loved, and working in a small town played a big role in that. During my time at this agency, I did get to know a lot of the locals and several of the visitors who would make their way into town a couple of times a week to gamble. There was also the chance to work closely with the firefighters, learning how to operate equipment and help them on fire scenes. They went as far as teaching me how to give someone an IV and hook them up to fluids. We spent many days eating dinner with them, watching football on Sundays, or playing station golf, which is like Putt-Putt but in a fire station. These were good times, working in a small town.

Traffic Stops

In the beginning, I enjoyed doing traffic stops; but as time went on, I grew to hate them unless I was bored and needed something to do. I enjoyed getting flashed by the female drivers in hopes of getting out of a speeding ticket and being propositioned so they wouldn't get arrested for driving drunk. One of my favorite stops was an older gal I pulled over who was speeding through a school zone. Speeding in a school or construction zone always got an automatic ticket from me.

When I first contacted her at the stop, she was friendly. I noticed she was wearing short shorts and a white half-shirt with nothing underneath. She was in her forties and not in bad shape. As I walked back to my patrol car to clear her driving status and complete a speeding ticket, I noticed she was moving around a lot in the front seat. It was not like she was reaching under the seat or looking for something, but more like she was trying to get comfortable sitting in the driver's seat or rearranging herself. I continued writing the ticket and watching what she was doing.

As I returned to the vehicle, which was a pickup truck, I noticed she had gone from having both feet on the floor and a normal sitting position to having her right leg still on the floor and her left leg brought up to where her foot was on the seat and knee up against the window. This was when the driver's license didn't have hair color on the driver's description, but I needed it for the ticket along with her phone number for court purposes. As I was standing next to the truck, I had a habit of slightly lowering my sunglasses and looking over the top of them, which made people nervous.

I asked her for her phone number so it could be added to her court records, which she provided. I then asked for natural hair color as needed for the ticket. At this time, she lowered her sunglasses, looked down at her crotch, back at me, and said, "Brown, naturally." As she stated this, I followed her eyes and noticed she had exposed her crotch in an attempt to get out of the ticket. Unfortunately, this didn't work in her favor.

She still got the ticket. But hey! I got a crotch shot, which made for a better, not-so-boring day. She even asked if there was anything she could do for me not to submit the ticket and instead tear it up. She stressed the word "anything." As tempting as this was, being a single guy in my mid-twenties, I remained strong and told her to have a better day while walking away before I got myself into trouble.

While running traffic during a night shift, I pulled over a carload of early twenty-something females. There were four in the car, and the stop was because the driver was speeding. As I approached the driver, I asked for a license, registration, and insurance, telling her the reason for the traffic stop. She was acting overly nice and even told me I had beautiful eyes. She was playing it up, but I didn't smell alcohol. I was thinking there was something else that was going to come up, like her driving with a suspended license or something. I ran clearance on her driving status, and she was valid. She wasn't going too much over the speed limit, but enough for me to pull her over and issue a warning.

As I approached the car again, I noticed all four females had exposed their breasts and were just sitting there with big smiles. "We are hoping this helps me not get a ticket," the driver said. Trying to be professional and not provide any reaction, I stated, "Ma'am, I wasn't going to give you a ticket anyway, but thank you for making this a better day. Have a good day yourself. Cover those up and drive safe for me." It's hard to have just another day on the job when a female exposes herself to get out of a ticket.

Not all traffic stops turned out with those results, although it happened a few times when I was younger. As I got older, people could apparently see I just didn't care, and I was told I looked mean and cranky. Maybe I did; I don't know. There were other weird traffic stops I would make. My rule was if a guy cried, it was an automatic ticket. It was common to see a girl crying to get out of a ticket. Whether a ticket was actually issued all depended on how fast they were going and the reason they were driving that way.

Getting flashed did not only happen with females. One time, I was flashed by a guy. As I was writing him a ticket for speeding, he was fiddling around in the driver's seat, but not in a concerning manner. He was fully exposed as I returned to the car, pants down around his knees and jerking off. He looked straight at me and stated, "You can help if you want. I wouldn't mind. Maybe it'll help me get out of that ticket in your hand." This fired me up quickly.

I told him he had better pull up his pants and stop stroking himself, or I would arrest him for public indecency and attempting to bribe a police officer. At least the females weren't rubbing themselves or performing sexual acts. They would just expose themselves. This sick bastard took it way too far.

After he pulled up his pants and covered himself, he started crying—not because he was sorry, but because he would lose his license and job with this ticket. Feeling no pity whatsoever, I told him I may have considered that, but any chance of getting out of the ticket was thrown out the window when he started doing what he was doing when I approached the car. I had no empathy for this sick idiot. You never know who or what you will pull over when doing a traffic stop.

As I said, the ticket depended on the speed at which someone traveled over the limit, except in a school or construction zone. Anything over fifteen miles over the speed limit was an automatic ticket, no matter the circumstance. I made a traffic stop on a guy speeding thirty miles per hour over the posted limit. When I spoke with him, he told me he was about to crap his pants and was just trying to get to the gas station before he did. I was empathetic to that, so I told him to give me license registration and insurance, and I would follow him to the gas station so he could use the bathroom, which I thought was kind and understanding.

While he was using the bathroom, I was preparing a ticket for speeding because he was in the range of receiving a ticket—well within the range. When he came out, I handed him the ticket and his items. He tried to get me not to write because of the situation, but my empathy only goes so far. I could have taken the chance and made him wait where I'd initially stopped him until I was done writing the ticket. He may not have needed the bathroom after that.

Being called racist was a common occurrence at traffic stops. At night, in the dark, through tinted windows, one cannot tell what race somebody is unless they have x-ray vision and can see through dark objects. On top of that, my radar device did not have a race setting to monitor. I pulled over everybody and anybody when I was actually out running traffic, which was not often—maybe a couple of times a month.

We did not have requirements on how many tickets to write or how many DUI arrests to make. Our chief didn't want us to run traffic; most people who came into town were tourists and there to spend money. I would constantly tell the chief, "Well, they are spending money, just in a different way than what they had in mind." The chief would just shake his head and walk away, mumbling to himself. He would say, "Not so much. The city council doesn't want to stop people coming into town that often." I really wouldn't learn about quotas until my next department.

Working Holidays

I had a rule for when I had to work during the holidays. My goal was to make an arrest on Christmas night to keep things interesting. This was effective every year I worked during the holidays except for one. Before I was married, I would let the officers with families have most holidays off so they could enjoy spending time with them.

I figured I didn't have kids or anything. I had a girlfriend, but nothing that would keep me from working holidays so that the other officers with families could take off. Besides that, I would get paid double time-and-a-half and gain an extra day to take off at another time. If a scuffle happened during an arrest, it made things even better. The paperwork and transport to the county jail kept me busier for longer. One year, we arrested a whole family—a father, a mother, and a son — for theft. A family who steals together also gets to spend Christmas in jail together!

They were pretty swift with their plan. Mom would locate a chair in the casino with a purse left unattended on it. She would then put her coat over the purse and chair and start gambling. Dad would show up a couple of minutes later. He would swap the chair with the coat and purse on it with another next to Mom. Dad would sit for a minute and then walk away empty-handed. Son would then come over to Mom. He would talk to her for a minute and then grab Mom's coat and purse and walk away, leaving Mom to her gambling. Son and Dad would meet up in another part of the casino where they would go through the purse, take out what they wanted, and dump the purse into a nearby trashcan.

We watched this happen on a surveillance camera. It appeared to have been going on for about six hours, with several victims being left behind. Of course, they didn't just do this all at one casino. They went through several casinos.

Somehow, they had caught the eye of a security officer, who advised the surveillance officer to watch these three on the camera and record their movements. After thirty minutes or so, they were seen doing the same thing they had in the other casinos. When the surveillance officer saw this, he immediately called us, and the other security officer detained them until we arrived.

Now, we are not talking about the smartest people in the crowd. They were getting away with it for several hours, but they didn't know they were under surveillance cameras the whole time. They were being surveilled no matter which casino they went to and where they were in the casino. Of course, they tried denying doing anything wrong. Mom insisted, "Oh, I didn't see the purse on the chair where I laid my coat." Dad was ready to throw Mom under the bus, "If she put her coat over someone else's purse, I had no idea. I was just moving her coat closer to her." And the son, the real genius of the three, kept saying, "I never felt a purse under Mom's coat. I was just told to take it with me. Dad and I never went through any purses. This all had to be Mom's doing."

Ah, the loving son and father to the mother who provided for them. I rarely show surveillance footage to the suspects before they go to court. However, I could not resist. I just wanted to see the reaction on their precious little Christmas-celebrating faces when they saw the evidence I had. Dad and Son were in one holding cell together, and Mom was in a holding cell right next to them. So, I rolled in the television and VCR and placed them in front of the cells where they could all watch the very interesting reality TV show they'd been starring in.

Once they started watching what they were doing in the casinos, the dad immediately blamed it on the son and mom, saying it was their idea and he was only being a supportive, loving father by helping them. The other two just remained quiet with their jaws on the floor. They couldn't believe they got caught and were going to jail on Christmas Day. They even asked if I could get them transported sooner so they could bond out and at least have some Christmas left. After laughing a little (okay, a lot), I made sure to hold them and not transport them until 11:59 p.m. on Christmas night. They'd ruined Christmas for plenty of other people, so I wasn't about to let them have any joy of their own.

Every year was something interesting. It was surprising how many people would be in town on Christmas, not spending time with family or even bringing the family with them. Most arrests on Christmas were family fights. Somebody didn't like dinner, or somebody would get drunk and decide to fight the rest. One year, we responded to a stabbing—a woman gave her husband a present of a steak knife in the gut! He had been out drinking all day and spending their money, not on gifts for her but on trying to win some at a casino.

He came home drunk. She had made a big dinner for the two of them. He didn't like it and told her how much he didn't like it. He also told her how bad of a cook she was in the first place and that she was getting nothing for Christmas because he'd spent all their money in a casino. She would have to pick up extra shifts so they could pay their bills. In return, she grabbed a steak knife off the dinner table and stuck him in the gut. She then called us to report the stabbing and to get an ambulance to her house. Ah, the joy of Christmas!

The police department and fire department would usually go in together and split the cost of a nice meal for the troops. There was always a firefighter willing to cook a Thanksgiving or Christmas dinner we would enjoy together. One year, I made a turkey dinner for my team and dispatch. It was a cheater meal, pre-bought, but it did the job. The pastor at a church next to the department let me use the stove there to heat everything up and take it to the station.

It was a good thing no calls for service came up, so nothing was burned. We never went without a meal when we worked one or both of these holidays. I always wanted to make sure everyone was able to enjoy a nice dinner, since the nights were mostly quiet until later in the evening after everybody had been drinking and the family fights had started. If the town was quiet all night, we would run traffic to see who we could bust on a DUI.

One Thanksgiving, while running traffic, I pulled over the mayor's son, who had been drinking all day—not around family, just hanging out at home drinking by himself. When I made the stop, I got the usual, "Do you know who I am?" I would always respond to this with, "Not yet, but I will shortly." Having never met this individual before, he wanted to make sure I knew he was the mayor's son and that I should probably just walk away and leave him alone.

He was heading to his mom and dad's for a turkey dinner, and he didn't want to miss a good, homecooked meal. He told me if I didn't let him just go to their house, he would make sure I was fired before the end of the shift. Bad news for him: I would have coffee with the mayor once every couple of weeks. I knew the mayor. I could smell the alcohol coming off his son's breath as soon as he started talking, so I knew this was not going to end well—for him.

I told him, "I don't care if you are the son of God, Jesus Christ. You are driving drunk in my town." After a few minutes of him continuing to threaten my job, I said, "Look, let me make sure you are okay to drive, because I can smell the alcohol. Get out of the vehicle and complete some roadside maneuvers, and if you pass, I will let you be on your way and make it in time for dinner." After he agreed to do so, I put him through some roadside tests to determine whether he was intoxicated. He was not even able to complete the tests because he kept falling over. I was afraid he was going to fall and crack his head open on the ground.

So, I arrested him for driving drunk and took him to the police station to complete some paperwork. My whole intention was to write him a ticket and drive him to his parent's house, but things can quickly change when someone is feeling ten feet tall and bulletproof. He continued to threaten my job. He wanted to make sure I understood he was going to have me fired and that he was the mayor's son.

When he realized his threats were not phasing me and I would not engage, he turned to threatening me physically.

He told me to take off the handcuffs so we could settle this "Mano-a-mano." I began chuckling at this invite to a physical fight, and he started growling at me like a bear. Eventually, I got tired of listening to his rants and threats and called his dad, the mayor, at home. I told the mayor about the threats and why I'd pulled him over. The mayor did not seem shocked by his son's actions. I was taken by surprise when the mayor then told me, "Take his ass to jail. I don't want him here, either. Let him know not to call me for bail. He can call one of his idiot friends."

The son heard this part of the conversation; he had stopped talking long enough to try to listen to what his dad was saying. He began crying uncontrollably like a child who'd just dropped his ice cream. I hate to see a grown man cry, but this time I enjoyed it. I'm not sure if he found anybody to bond him out or not, but I never received a subpoena for court. I hope he learned a hard lesson that I didn't care about his or anyone's status. I would arrest anybody, even on the holidays.

Sometimes, It's All Worth It

Then there were the calls that reminded me why I started the job. There was a child abuse case of seven-year-old twins where the mother had pinched the arms of one of the twins to teach her a lesson. It wouldn't have been so bad if there'd been only a few marks on the girl, but there were over thirty pinch marks on this little girl's arm. The child advised she had been pinching her sister, and their mother had gotten tired of it and began pinching her, all while saying, "You like how that feels?"

Both sisters were in the room together. A social services worker was with me during the interview, which took place at their school. When I asked her sister if there was anything else that had happened, I was told that their mom's boyfriend had made the other sister sit on a hot space heater once because she wouldn't stay away from the heater. This had happened approximately one year earlier, and it was apparent that the child had scars that had been made by the grate of a space heater.

I was furious that a mother would allow her children to live around garbage like this boyfriend. I immediately went to their mom's job and completed an interview with her. Mom admitted she had pinched the one girl to teach her a lesson for pinching her sister. She also admitted the boyfriend made the other girl sit on a hot space heater to teach her a lesson. Mom then told me, "I was investigated several times for child abuse in California, and nothing ever happened to me."

After this statement, I left the casino. The social service worker told me, "You know what you need to do. My report will be done by the end of business." So, I waited until the mom was walking out of work from her shift and placed her into custody for felony child abuse in the doorway of her job. I let her know why she was being arrested in a loud manner so everybody, including her boss and coworkers, could hear.

When the boyfriend got home later that night, he was arrested for felony child abuse, too. The girls were placed with their grandfather while their mom served seven years in prison. Grandpa did get full custody of both girls, and Mom lost all rights due to the crime committed against them. This was a great ending to a shitty case. It was the best possible outcome.

Although this was a one-square-mile town, people seemed to think they could hide easily or that there wasn't much that happened in the town. We had homicides, attempted homicides, and those wanted for crimes committed across several state lines. One such call consisted of a couple who had driven across five different states stealing mail out of mailboxes, looking for money, credit cards, or anything they could trade in for cash. They had also been involved in several burglaries.

We caught them when they slipped up and tried to sleep in their vehicle next to one of the casinos. The casino was closed, and signs were clearly posted to have all vehicles removed after closing time. When a couple of graveyard officers approached the vehicle, they observed a male and female sleeping inside it.

The officers also noticed several mail items in the vehicle, prompting them to call the detectives in at four in the morning. I was on light duty and working with the detectives at the time, so they called me in, as well. This couple would not say much of anything except that all the items in the vehicle belonged to them. Throughout their travels, according to them, they had found all of it along the road and in trash cans. You know, "finders, keepers."

During a search of the vehicle, several hundred pieces of mail were located crossing five different states and more than one hundred victims. The couple had also kept the items from the burglaries they'd committed. The vehicle was packed full of stolen goods. They admitted they had stopped in this town because they didn't believe they would be caught. They'd thought it was a small enough town to hide in and assumed the cops would be untrained and inexperienced.

Since I was the rookie detective at the time, it was my job to contact all the agencies in each city, town, and county the couple had traveled through. The next day, when I got back to work, the first thing I did was start calling over fifty agencies to determine whether they had any reports about burglaries and stolen mail. Around thirty-five departments had reports filed during the period and the travel route of these two fine, upstanding citizens.

While working with the other agencies to determine charges, items stolen, and victims, I was contacted by the Federal Bureau of Investigation. They were letting me know a couple of the other departments had contacted them, and since the crime spree ran across state lines, they would take over the case. My sergeant and I were happy to allow them to, since it was such a big case with so much involved, the reports were getting complicated, and the whole thing was a pain in the ass.

This was not the only instance when some government organization took over one of my cases. I had been dispatched to one of the casinos because an individual was trying to cash a check on which he had forged a signature. I was called because the cashier thought the check looked like it had been washed, and the original pay-to section was erased and written over. The cashier did a great job of keeping the suspect at the counter until I arrived at the casino.

I made contact with the suspect and asked to see the check he was trying to cash, which, without hesitation, he handed over to me. He said it was payment for a job he did for the person the account belonged to. At the same time, a Division of Gaming agent, who was considered a check fraud expert and damn good at it, arrived. I handed him the check and asked the agent to see what he thought. After some minutes of looking at it from different angles and in different lighting, he showed me who the check was originally made out to, which was not the suspect.

During further investigation, I was advised by the cashier that this individual had been in several times before attempting to cash checks and was turned away because they looked suspicious. After I placed the suspect into custody and transported him to the department, he was placed in a holding cell. I knew I had more work to do. After I dropped him off, I started going to all the other casinos to see if he could be located on surveillance footage cashing checks. During this investigation, some of the casinos still had the checks in their possession, as they had not yet been deposited.

After collecting all the checks, the gaming agent did the same thing as earlier. He looked at all the checks and determined they had all been forged. the "Pay to the Order of" sections had all been somehow erased, and his name was placed into that section to appear as if he had been the recipient of the checks. Within thirty days, the suspect had written checks for over $150,000, with several victims involved. While searching his vehicle, I located twenty-two different checkbooks, all having different victims' names on them.

During the booking process of the suspect, I found he was a Sergeant Major in the Army and less than sixty days from retirement after having served twenty-five years. His retirement was apparently not good enough for him. He was trying to get more to live up to the lifestyle he had made for himself. Unfortunately, he was just about to lose everything he'd worked for; he was charged with check fraud, felony style.

Three weeks after I took on this case, I received a call from the Military Police, who advised that the case had been transferred to one of the federal agencies because the suspect was military personnel and asked if I minded if they took it over. I was told the sentence he would get through the military would be tougher than any civilian court, and that he would end up serving his whole term. Of course I agreed to this—another case I didn't have to go to court on. The suspect ended up getting a sentence of fifteen years in a military prison.

You Never Know What Will Happen

When you return to work after your days off, you never know what might have happened while you were gone. Nothing has ever seemed to surprise me, though. After returning from one set of days off, I learned a friend and coworker, Officer Marin, was involved in a situation with an individual who was pissed off about a drunk driving charge and wanted to kill a cop in the town he was arrested in—this town.

The suspect had been driving around town for several hours, slowing down to look into the windows of businesses and sitting outside the gas station just staring inside from his vehicle. It was assumed he was hoping for one of the on-duty officers to be inside one of the businesses or to show up at the gas station to get a cup of coffee. Eventually, the clerk at the gas station called the police station, reporting the suspicious behavior, which occurred several times throughout the night. Officer Marin had taken the call and advised he would go check it out, but when he got to the gas station, the suspect had already left again. Officer Marin then decided to drive around and look for the vehicle.

After several minutes, he located it and started to follow it back toward the gas station. The vehicle began driving slowly once Officer Marin got behind him, and now he thought the driver was just drunk. Officer Marin hit his overhead emergency lights and attempted to make the traffic stop while the suspect was pulling into the gas station again. Officer Marin sat in his vehicle for a few more seconds just to see what the driver was going to do; he couldn't see into the vehicle to know what the driver was doing and was not sure the driver would get out.

Officer Marin then decided to go ahead and make contact. As he approached the vehicle, he started to walk wide to the driver's side—again, because he couldn't see inside. While walking toward the driver's side window, he could see the driver moving his head around as if looking for Officer Marin. As Officer Marin got close to the driver's window, he heard a sudden, muffled pop come from inside the vehicle. He told me later it sounded like a toy cap gun or firecracker going off in the vehicle. He said after he heard the pop, all he saw was a pink mist inside the vehicle, and the window turned red instantly like someone had just thrown paint against it.

As Officer Marin got to the window and could see into the vehicle, he realized the driver had shot himself and was missing part of his head. There was a lot of blood on the side window and ceiling. During the investigation following the traffic stop, it was learned the suspect had been arrested the night before for a drunk driving charge. According to his wife, he thought the arrest ruined his life, so he was going to get his vengeance.

It appeared when the traffic stop was made, the suspect attempted to get a shotgun from the passenger side. The suspect wanted to shoot Officer Marin when he approached the window. However, one thing went wrong: The driver grabbed the shotgun by the barrel with the rear stock on the floor beside a small toolbox, where it got caught. Apparently, when he jerked the shotgun to get the shotgun unstuck, the motion caused the shotgun to fire while the barrel was directed toward the side of the suspect's head. Officer Marin and the on-duty sergeant decided to consider this a self-correcting problem and completed the paperwork as suicide. We came close to losing an officer during this stop; however, karma took hold.

It seemed strange how shit always happened on my days off. People who get arrested for child sex assault end up going just a little bit crazy; trying to set the police department and patrol cars on fire apparently sounded like a great way for them to get even for being arrested. During a short leave of absence from work, I heard one of our officers was involved in a shooting outside the police station.

A guy had been arrested the night before for sexually assaulting a teenage girl and thought the arrest had ruined his career (that's right—the arrest, not the assault itself). He specifically blamed the officers who arrested him. The next night, the suspect decided to drive back into town in a pickup truck with one of those tanks in the bed of his truck used for filling gas tanks in big road equipment like front-end loaders. Using the nozzle of the gas tank, he turned it into a flame thrower while sitting in the cab of his truck. The hose was long enough to run in through the back window and out the driver's side window.

Dispatch saw it via video cameras on the outside of the building; all they could make out was this guy sitting in his truck trying to catch the cars on fire with his "flamethrower." From the way I understand, there was only one dispatcher inside the building at the time, and an officer inside visiting and taking a short break. The dispatcher and officer went out the side door of the department. By the time they got outside, the suspect was trying to set the brick building on fire because the cars apparently wouldn't burn.

As they walked around the outside the building, the flame was directed toward them. The dispatcher dove behind one of the cars, and the officer opened fire into the driver's side of the truck. Seeing the video footage, I found the shooting pretty impressive. The officer had fired seven rounds into the driver's side door, following the body of the suspect. All seven shots struck the driver, neutralizing that threat. While I worked for the department, this was the only officer-involved shooting our agency had been involved in; there may have been some in the past, however.

When dealing with off-duty law enforcement who would come to our town, the majority knew how to act professionally and respect the town they were visiting. However, there were times when we'd come across some who'd decided getting drunk and acting foolish would be a great idea. They also thought they wouldn't get arrested. WRONG! We had been called to an intoxicated party who turned out to be an off-duty U.S. Marshal, and he was getting belligerent with security at one of the businesses.

When we arrived on the scene, he had identified himself as a U.S. Marshal to half the business but had calmed down considerably. Security advised they didn't want him arrested but that he needed to be cut off from drinking and get a hotel room to sleep off the drunk. After talking with the Marshal, he agreed to get a room and go to bed. He decided it would be better than getting arrested and dealing with his supervisor the next day. Unfortunately, this lasted only a few hours, and then he was back at it with security. Instead of waiting for us to get there, he decided he would just drive home and not come back—or so he stated.

Security watched him walk to his car and tried to stop him from driving away. He could barely stand, and his speech was slurred; only God knows what made him think he could drive. After he tried to run over the security officers, they decided to back away and let him go. They were afraid they were going to get hurt, and they didn't get paid enough for that. When we got to the parking lot, security gave us the information and details on his vehicle, and we went to make the stop before he killed somebody.

He didn't get far. He'd made it less than a mile up the road before we saw him and made the traffic stop. We thought he would just go back to the hotel instead of getting arrested and ruining his career, but alcohol makes supermen out of stupid people. When he came to a stop, he put his car in park and exited from the driver's side door. After taking a drink, he stood up, slammed an open beer can on the top of his vehicle, and stated, "I am a U.S. Marshal. You know you can't do shit to me. Besides, professional courtesy may favor you in the future!" I thought, "What the fuck is wrong with this guy? What favor would I, or we, need from him?"

My partner and I then looked at each other. Then, with a grin on his face, my partner walked over to the Marshal and said, "You fucked up any chance you had when you left, dumbass. Now, you get to go to jail." The Marshal tried to resist being placed in handcuffs by locking his hands together in front of him, but after breaking his grip, we got the cuffs on—and yes, he was fully booked into jail with charges. Since we never got a subpoena to appear in court on this case, it is unsure as to what happened to him.

Another time, a group of correctional officers thought they could come to town and cause a scene after getting drunk. They also thought that since they worked for the state prison system, they had authority over us and could tell us what we could and could not do. Closing time was coming, and our officers were trying to get everyone out of the establishment. Since drinking ends at two in the morning, security has a right to take someone's alcoholic drink away from them and escort them to their awaiting bus to send them home and out of town.

Well, these two upstanding members of the law enforcement community started harassing the security officers. They pulled out their badges and told security if anybody touched them, it would be considered an assault on the officers, and they would make sure everyone was charged. Again, these were correctional officers with no charging capabilities outside the facility where they worked. Security, however, was unsure how to respond and was a little intimidated, so we were called to deal with these two morons.

When we arrived on the scene, the bus was still waiting for them as instructed by security, but these two would not get on the bus and were demanding they finish their drinks before leaving town. They even spoke to my partner and me as if we worked under them and they were our supervisors, telling us not to touch them and that we needed to just mind our own business. They even went as far as telling us they would press charges through the state if we laid hands on them.

Lo and behold! We had someone with us who personally knew the warden of the facility they worked at and had a home phone number to call, and it was now two-thirty in the morning. So, Officer Ferring made a phone call to the house number of the warden, their boss, who could hear them yelling and demanding their drinks in the background. Officer Ferring informed the warden of why he was calling and how his officers' actions were affecting the closing of the business. He also let the warden know that these two were about to be arrested for disorderly conduct.

After telling the warden about the incident, Officer Ferring handed the phone to one of the correctional officers and said, "He wants to talk to you." The officer said, "Who the fuck wants to talk to me, and why would I care?" Officer Ferring said, "It's your boss, and you may want to take this right now." Once Officer Ferring handed the drunk officer his phone, all we heard was, "Yes, sir. I understand, sir." And "Your office Monday morning? Yes, sir. We will be there."

He then hung up the phone, looked at his buddy, and said, "Shut the fuck up and get on the bus. This is not good." As they got on the bus, the officer who'd taken the phone call said, "If it helps, I apologize for both of us. We were out of line." His partner had said something inaudible on the bus, and this one turned toward him and again yelled, "Shut the fuck up, asshole! We are in enough trouble!" It does pay to know people in high places. The two of them left, and we never got a visit from them again.

Then, there were the strange things we'd find in people's houses while searching for drugs, stolen property, or whatever was being searched for under a warrant. Porn seemed to be the common thing owned amongst criminals—not the kind you buy, but home videos and photos. It never failed: Whenever we would execute a search warrant on a house, someone always came across the homemade porn videos or pictures, and it was always in the underwear drawer. It was never a guess on the videos, either. They were always marked with handwritten titles like "Sex" or "A Good Fucking" with the dates they were made, or some other kind of note so they wouldn't forget what was on the videos. I suppose showing the family your vacation videos and pulling out the wrong one could be a little embarrassing.

There were many search warrants executed on many different houses. We had a drug dealer who apparently enjoyed trading sex for drugs—not uncommon, I know. However, his video and photo collection were impressive. As we searched through his house, we began finding photos of some of the local women in town who you would never suspect as drug users. They were clean, married, and had children.

It was a real surprise when we found one involving a city council member. Not only was she having sex with this guy, but we found a photograph of her involving a baseball bat, and it was sticking out of her butt, big end in first. I could never look at her the same or take her seriously after this finding, especially after we contacted her asking what she was doing at the residence and asking to search her place for narcotics. She gave consent to search, and while we were searching, we slipped the photograph into a location where she would find it quickly—her underwear drawer. Nothing was ever said. We knew she found it; she just could not look us in the eye from that day forward.

Of course, we always had to watch the videos to make sure there was no evidence of wrongdoing, such as active drug use or anybody involved who was underage. Out of all the drug warrants we executed, we did come across one individual who had his own collection of porn, again homemade. He was a 350-pound drug dealer, but he didn't sell to adults; he was selling to teenagers, and those teenagers had to pay him somehow. Since he was making his own meth in the bathtub, he was taking payment either way.

While searching his house and knowing he was selling to teenagers, we came across a lot of videos marked only with a date. As we started watching the videos to see what was on them, we realized he was making porn videos with underage kids, both boys and girls. We further learned

190

this sick piece of shit would only take sex for drugs. He wanted no money, and if the kids wanted drugs from him, they knew they would have to have sex with this fat tub of lard. Apparently, this was the only way he could get laid.

Getting sicker by the minute, now we had to identify all these kids in these videos. He had about fifteen videos in his collection. Some of the kids were the same, so there were only about eight victims involved—which of course was eight too many. Again, you never know what you will find in people's homes, and if we hadn't completed a search warrant on this fat bastard's house, we might have never known about these victims of sexual assault. Drugs make people do crazy shit.

Speaking of juveniles having sex, one would think if they knew everybody was getting caught having sex in a specific location, maybe they would choose not to have sex there. But no, that is not how kids' minds work. They are just looking for a dark spot outside of their parents' house to get intimate with one another. It never failed. The one spot overlooking the city was where they would all go. It was right on the edge of city limits with no nearby houses, so when a car was seen at this location, it was considered odd.

About once every few months, while working the night shift, we would patrol that area to see who was hanging out. Often, I would notice a vehicle parked, lights out, windows fogged, and the car rocking. I would pull up, blacked out and slow, trying not to catch the attention of the kids in the car. As soon as I would get right behind the vehicle, I would turn on my overhead emergency lights and hit the siren. Both people would jump since the lights scared the hell out of them. They would try to scramble and get their clothes back on.

I never saw anything more than their heads and would allow them to get dressed while I waited. But there were a lot of people in town who knew something was happening at this overlook; they could see the lights, and the siren echoed. One boy and his girlfriend were caught several times by different officers. I had known her dad for many years. He didn't know it was happening until after they took her home and the boy was gone.

The problem was that he had no idea who the boyfriend was, either. Nobody would provide that information to the dad. Being a father of girls myself, I knew it was maddening for him not to know, so when I came across his daughter this last time, I made a phone call. He would have to come get her, anyway. I also called the boy's parents, since I was assuming they had no idea what he was up to, either. The boy's mother was the first to arrive, and she was pissed. It had been a long time since I had seen someone being led by the ear, but she grabbed hold of this kid's ear and twisted it, dragging him to his knees.

About the time he hit the ground, the girl's father pulled up. I knew he was upset. When he got out of his vehicle, the first words out his mouth were, "Where the fuck is the little son of a bitch who's having sex with my daughter?" I thought he was going to kill this kid until he saw that his mom had him on his knees, and that he was begging her to let go of that one ear. Dad calmed down quickly toward the boy; however, the girl was still in a world of trouble. He grabbed hold of her arm, forced her into his vehicle, and off they drove without saying anything further. On the other hand, the boyfriend's mom had plenty to say to him, including cutting off his pecker if she ever had to deal with this again. Once she was done yelling at him, she let him get back into his car to drive it home, where it stayed parked for the remainder of the school year.

Kids weren't the only people who were caught having sex in this spot. We had plenty of adults, some married and cheating on their spouses with their secret lovers or coworkers. Unlike the juveniles. whenever I would hit my overhead emergency lights and sirens, it was always the female who would pop up from the back seat wearing nothing but a surprised look on her face. It never failed. I saw more boobs through the back window of vehicles than I can count.

I would have to say one of the funniest calls I went on was the report of someone throwing their shoes at people on the sidewalk and in the street. When we arrived on the scene, we noticed a male throwing a shoe at a female while calling her a slut in a high-pitched voice and talking about how he could make her husband happier than she could. He would then run and grab his shoe to throw at someone else. He was a gay male who'd apparently had way too much to drink that night and was getting turned down by the other guys he was hitting on.

When I got out of my car, he saw me and started yelling, "You can't catch me, bitches!" and began running away from us after slipping his shoes back on. As he was running, he kept looking over his left and right shoulders, trying to keep an eye on us. He was not paying attention to where he was actually running. Of course, we gave chase on foot but didn't have to run far, as he crashed into the wrought iron handrail that separated the upper and lower section of the sidewalk while running at a full sprint. The fence was about waist-high, and the impact caused him to complete a full flip over the handrail, landing on his back. He hit the ground with such force that his shoes flew off his feet, one landing on the roof of a nearby businesses. I immediately stopped in my tracks and began laughing so hard I could not move, and from the lower sidewalk section, I could hear him yelling, "Okay bitches, I guess you *can* catch me." When I was done laughing, along with everybody else who saw this happen, I took him into custody and transported him to our holding cells, where I was just going to write him a ticket and put him on a bus out of town so he could go home. But his shenanigans did not stop there.

Once he was able to breathe again and focus, he decided messing with the cameras in the jail cell was in his best interest. While we were working on paperwork and completing our reports, we were called into dispatch, where surveillance cameras could be viewed. All we were told was, "You may want to come and see this." When we walked into dispatch and looked at the screen, we were just in time to see him smear poop on the camera, and he was naked from the waist down.

He then yelled, "Now you can't see anything, bitches!" and he began masturbating, not something you really want to deal with toward the end of the shift, and who was going in to deal with this? That's right, me. I had to go in and stop him from masturbating and place him back into handcuffs with his shit-covered hands. So, in I go, wearing latex gloves and having to wrestle him to the ground— and by the way: GROSS! After breaking his grip on his junk, I was able to get him into cuffs. No bus ride was in his future after this—just a free ride to the jail to bond out from there.

I always considered myself on duty all the time, whether I was working or not. There were times I stopped at traffic accidents to assist. I would get involved with assaults or domestics, as well. Whatever crime was happening while I was around, I made sure to assist. This work ethic and my being on the SWAT team were reasons enough for me not to drink a lot of alcohol on my days off. I had the occasional beer, but not too often.

I also never bragged or talked much about the things I did that would get officers acknowledged, such as stopping for traffic accidents or covering another officer on my way home. For example, while driving to work one evening, I passed a car off the side of the road on fire, so I decided to stop and make sure there was nobody inside. When I made my way down, I noticed the driver was unconscious behind the wheel. The fire was in the engine compartment and contained for the moment. Another car stopped because they'd noticed the flames as well.

Together, we were able to get the driver out of the car before it was fully engulfed in flames. This was the first time I learned just how fast the rest of a car catches fire once one of the doors is opened. I've given CPR to people before rescue arrived and been able to bring some back. I've lost some, too. I knew officers who would make sure these deeds were noticed and acknowledged by telling the chief or their supervisor, all because they wanted the little medal they would receive, their fame and glory.

My supervisors knew what I had done through word of mouth from other agencies, and when they would say something, I would just tell them it was part of the job, and I didn't need to be recognized for anything special. I was not doing the job for recognition; I was doing the job because I wanted to and just did what was expected of me. That came from being taught by officers who had been doing the job a lot longer than I had: just do your job and shut the hell up. Medals don't make the officer. Your actions do.

The Lighter Side

At some point during the shift, you need to let loose and have some fun. One way we would have fun was playing tricks on each other or scaring the rookies who were fresh out of field training. Sometimes, we would stay after shift and be in cahoots with dispatch and the other officer working that night. Then we would head to the cemetery on the outskirts of town and get things set up before dispatch would send the rookie out to check on some strange occurrence happening in the cemetery grounds.

One night, a few of us got off shift and headed out. We were working on a new guy who claimed nothing scared him and that he didn't believe in ghosts or the supernatural. We strung a line between a couple of trees within an aspen grove and tied a white sheet onto a makeshift zipline. With enough of a slope downhill, this sheet looked like an apparition moving through the trees at a distance. We then set up a boom box and put in a cassette tape of a woman screaming. It had been recorded earlier in the day; the woman was the day-shift dispatcher, and her screams were enough to send chills down your spine.

Once we were set up, three of us hid behind headstones throughout the cemetery and called into dispatch on a channel not monitored by the on-duty officers that we were ready for the new guy to be sent to the cemetery. Using the excuse that a suspicious party was wandering through the cemetery, two officers in their cars were dispatched out. Only one knew what was going down. As they entered the area, the rookie continued further into the cemetery to look for this suspicious party. As he reached the beginning of the headstones and where the "ghost" could be seen, the recorder was turned on, and a scream flowed across the cemetery, causing him to look in the direction of the trees. Right after the scream, as he was heading toward the trees, the "ghost" was released, flowing across the trees, looking like a ghost in flight.

The rookie started yelling into the radio that he saw something in white running through the trees and calling for the other car to come to his location. Acting like he didn't hear, the other officer stayed in his car close to the entrance, and the rookie continued moving toward the tree line. About that time, one of the other off-duty officers ran through the cemetery, causing the rookie to head in another direction in his vehicle, which was coming toward me at this point. I was perched behind a headstone looking like a tree, waiting until he got close.

As the front of his vehicle started passing the headstone, I jumped out and onto the hood. The rookie let out this high-pitched scream, slamming on the brakes and rolling out of the driver's side while still screaming. As he hit the ground, he started crawling backward to get away from what had just jumped out at him: me. I immediately started laughing at his reaction, which caught his attention, and he was able to get to his feet. Madder than hell, he called me several not-so-nice names and sped out of the cemetery.

After the rest of us cleaned everything up and gathered our stuff, we returned to the department to ensure he was okay and hadn't pissed himself. It took him some time, but he was able to calm down, vowing never to go into the cemetery again—because the one thing we did not tell him was fake was the "ghost" flying through the trees. He asked several times if we had seen it and what it was. We had him thoroughly convinced the cemetery was haunted and that he was the only witness.

There were times when the snow would come down so heavy the state would close the roads, both into and out of town. What does a day-shift officer do when they are stuck in town and don't have to work because their relief got in right before the roads were closed? Well, party—that's what you do! On one of these snowy nights, the town was dead; there was hardly anybody around, and those who lived there were settled in at home.

My day shift partner decided to drive through town, telling everybody we were having a blizzard party at one of the local bars. Having a hotel room for the night across the street made it easy not to drive after the shift ended, and we packed that bar. The bar owner was happy to make some money on such a crappy night. We had a detective at the time who was secretly dating one of the local women in town but trying hard to keep it a secret as to who she was or where she lived, to the point he would cover his car so it wasn't noticed by somebody driving by.

However, this night was different for some reason. He took a patrol car to her house, where he was spending the night, and left it outside and uncovered. The night shift sergeant drove by and noticed it was the patrol vehicle assigned to this officer. What does a sergeant do when something like that is noticed, knowing the officer is trying to keep it a secret? He tells the others that he is still in town and partying at the local bar.

In our not-so-shining moment, the sergeant gave two of us a ride to where the car was located. Since all the cars were keyed the same and we each had our own set of keys, we stole the car out of the driveway, rolling backward so we didn't wake him up and starting it once we got it into the street. As the vehicle's driver, I thought it would be even funnier to park it at the chief's house in the middle of the night. We then returned to the bar, closed our tab, and left so we could get some sleep before our shift started again in four hours. Arriving at the office the next day, we waited for the officer to come strolling into work.

When he finally arrived, I asked him why he was running late, knowing he'd had to walk from across town. All he said was, "You guys are fucking hilarious." Acting like we had no idea what he was talking about, I asked where his patrol car was. He stated, "Wherever you assholes put it. I don't know where it is." Now, this was an opening to continue messing with him and plant a little seed of panic. He was an egotistical jackass at times. So, I advised him we did nothing with his car, and we were with several people at the bar in town who could verify we were there, including the bartender and owner. They would both vouch for us if he wanted to check.

The panic I'd been hoping to cause suddenly washed over his face. Now, he really thought the patrol car had been stolen and was worried he'd have to explain to his sergeant why he was parked at this girl's house. He still didn't want anybody to know he was dating her. We had him going for over an hour; he was panicking about how to explain this. At the same time, the chief came strolling into the office. Somehow, he always knew I was involved in the shenanigans.

He said, "Russell, not sure how that car got in my driveway, and I don't want to know how or why. Just make sure it gets moved before I get home." The officer heard this from down the hall and started throwing things in his office—having a fit, if you will. He came to my office and told me to take him to his car and that I was an asshole. Well, what do you do when someone calls you an asshole? You make his ass walk to get his own car and let him know the town is too small to hide his little secret love affairs.

We had a female detective who would come into work angry every morning and did not like to be talked to for the first hour she was there. But, being unable to help myself, if I was in the office, I would say, "Good morning, Sunshine." Her response every time was, "Fuck you, Ford," before continuing into her office and slamming the door. This went on for about six months before my sergeant decided we needed to teach her a lesson and not to be so mean every morning. With that in mind, we went to a local store and found some stink bombs. One morning, before she came into work, we taped two packets of the stink bombs to the inside frame of the door so that when she slammed it shut, they would break open. What we didn't realize was how bad these things truly were.

As she walked in, I did my normal, "Good morning, Sunshine," and it was followed by her normal response: "Fuck you, Ford!" She stomped down the hall into her office and slammed the door. About five minutes later, my sergeant and I could smell the results of the stink bomb. We then heard her coughing and gagging inside her office, yelling, "What the fuck is that?" It's hard to laugh and not breathe at the same time. The sarge and I ran out the back door, realizing we'd stunk up the whole upstairs of the department.

As she came running out the back door, too, she quickly realized who was responsible for this prank. All we could tell her was that she ought not to be so quick to slam the door every morning. You never know what may be on the other side. We all learned a lesson that day. She could throw a pretty good punch, and she needed not to come in so angry every morning; after all, a person's attitude determines the price they pay.

Other pranks may have involved dead animals being placed in cars and fireworks being launched toward each other from the tops of buildings. But nothing can beat picking on the shortest guy in the department. Jim served as a Marine Corps drill instructor for several years. He loved wearing the Mounty hats, the ones with the flat brims he used to wear as a DI. Jim was only five feet tall but had the ego of a giant; however, he could take the joking pretty well and often made fun of himself. Since he liked wearing these hats, he convinced the chief to allow us to order some and wear them on duty. They are intimidating to the common citizen when worn low with a pair of sunglasses.

He made a traffic stop of a tall pickup truck one day. As he exited his vehicle, he made sure to put the hat on. I was his cover for this stop and was standing on the passenger side toward the back of the truck when Jim walked up to speak with the driver. All you could see was the bobbing up and down of this Mounty hat. Jim was short enough that you couldn't even see the top of his head, but the hat made him look taller. He approached the driver, who was obviously expecting someone a little taller, and jumped when Jim started talking to him.

The driver stated, "Holy shit, son, you scared the hell out of me. I didn't even see you walking to the car! Which of the Seven Dwarfs are you?" As Jim began turning red and getting angry, he noticed me chuckling a little about the comment and realized it wasn't worth getting upset over. We had placed stacked phone books in his patrol vehicle and a booster seat at one time. He always laughed about it and would make some smart-ass remark.

One day, Jim and I had to search for a suspect in a tight area. As we were walking through a hallway, I didn't notice the low-hanging ceiling and smacked my head. With a grin on his face, he turned and said, "That is why it is worth being short. Nothing hangs this low." I stopped making fun of him after that.

Sometimes, the Bad Ones Slip Through

For many years, I worked with an officer who was as egotistical as the day is long. He thought he was Hercules himself. Rob was one of those who turned out to be a not-so-good officer. Sure, he could hold his own and was always there to cover you; but he was also the first one to start hitting on a victim and trying to get her to sleep with him.

Even though he was married, he had one affair after another, always telling his wife he was working when not scheduled or lying about working late. This caused him big trouble when she called looking for him one night, and I answered the phone. When she asked to speak with Rob, I told her he wasn't working.

She told me he'd told her he was working late, and she needed to get hold of him because there was an issue with their son. Again, I told her he was not working and had left several hours prior. Next thing we knew, he came in to work and shared that his wife had left him. In return, he found another girlfriend. I guess he did that to help with the grieving process.

Rob was a gym rat, a muscle-head, and was always working out. He knew, or at least believed, he was the perfect specimen and the best-looking man in the room, and he would tell you so. He could not walk by a mirror without looking at himself. Sometimes, he would even stop and pose. He wore tight t-shirts so he could show off his physique when he came to work or left his shift. He would say, "The women like it, and the men want to be me."

One day, Rob, a dispatcher, and I were heading up some stairs for a break. Rob was in front of the dispatcher and me. Jokingly, I told the dispatcher to stop looking at Rob's ass. She laughed and stated he wasn't her type. Rob turned around and stated, "If she's not looking at my ass, she's the only one." He continued walking up the stairs. We rolled our eyes at his statement, but this was how egotistical he could be.

What we didn't know was the underlying sex issues he had. Rob turned out to be a pervert. One day, our female detective was using the bathroom, which was also the locker room in the building, consisting of a shower, a sink, and several lockers that faced the toilet. There was no separation between the rooms, so when someone was taking a shower, changing, or using the toilet, you had to lock the main door so nobody else could come in. It caused some to be late, as they had to wait for others to finish getting cleaned up or using the bathroom.

Anyway, while this female detective was using the toilet, she noticed a small red light coming out of Rob's locker directly in front of the toilet. When she finished, she started to investigate further and realized it was a video camera pointing toward the toilet. We were not sure how long this had been there. When the chief came in, she notified him of what she'd found, and they opened Rob's locker to see if the video camera was recording.

Once they retrieved the camera and reviewed its contents, they learned it had been recording throughout the night from when he got off his shift. He had been videotaping people using the toilet. Rob apparently had some fetish, and he had recorded everybody. He was terminated shortly after the investigation, but no charges were brought forward, as the Assistant District Attorney did not think there was enough evidence at the time. If I understood it correctly, Rob stated he accidentally left it running, and it just happened to be pointing at the toilet.

Apparently, abusing your spouse was okay if you thought you wouldn't get caught. Officer Hunch was assigned to a special unit working with officers from other departments in the same county. This was a special domestic violence unit. I had learned this officer had physically abused his wife on multiple occasions, and the final time was right before he was sent out of state to training.

His wife had confided in me that they had gotten into an argument before he left for this training. She told me he accused her of cheating on him, and as the argument progressed, he took off a belt he was wearing and began striking her on her back with it. She reluctantly showed me her back where she'd been hit. The welts and marks were still present, along with abrasions left from the belt. Knowing I could be in trouble if I said nothing and he then did something worse to her, I did not sleep much that night. I was not sure what should be done.

Okay. I knew what had to be done, but I didn't want to be the department snitch. I was between a rock and a hard place, and nobody was there to help me with my decision, or so I thought. I knew she needed to be protected. If he was willing to use a belt on her this time, what would be next? That thought bothered the shit out of me.

The next morning, when I got to work, Sgt. Riker and I decided to walk around the casinos and grab some breakfast afterward. I think he knew something was off with me and wanted to ensure I was okay. I told Riker I was fine and just had some stuff on my mind. After a little more prodding, I decided to ask Sgt. Riker's advice in a hypothetical way—as in, if there was an officer who did this, how would you react and respond?

Sgt. Riker told me exactly what he would do and said he wouldn't care about the thoughts of others; we are there to protect the innocent and those who cannot defend themselves. He finally asked me what was going on and why I was asking him this "hypothetical" question. Feeling comfortable, I told him what I had learned and observed. After all, Hunch was an egotistical asshole, anyway. I let Sgt. Riker know that the victim had shown me her injuries; based on my experience, I believed they were recent—maybe a couple of days old.

Sgt. Riker advised me he would take things over from here and wouldn't let anybody know right away who'd told him. He said just to let it go for now. After breakfast, Sgt. Riker disappeared into his office for quite some time, which I learned is when he contacted the rest of Hunch's team and filled them in on the situation. During the investigation, I learned more officers had the same type of information and reports. The problem was that they'd also been afraid to report it.

After the investigation, which took a few days, Hunch was due to return from his training; he was flying into a nearby airport. As he got out of the plane and into the terminal, the rest of the team was standing there waiting for him. He thought this was a welcoming committee for his return. I heard he was smiling when he saw them—but not for long, as he was arrested right there in the airport and charged with domestic violence. During the trial, seven officers testified against him, along with several other witnesses.

The evidence was overwhelming; however, the jury decided to acquit Hunch because they were afraid other officers would retaliate against them if he were found guilty. Sometimes, it just amazed me how stupid jurors could be. He was able to walk away with no charges. The good thing was that his career still ended. The chief fired him as soon as he was charged. We found out later that his wife had left him and moved to another state where he couldn't find her.

Small towns are good for people to come to work in when there isn't a thorough background investigation completed. The worst thing for any law enforcement officer is social media. Of course, we're all allowed to post whatever we want by the First Amendment, which states we have the right to free speech. One officer would call in sick to work at least once a month. After about a year of this, we were able to locate his social media page, which was not locked down. We always had a record of when people used sick time or took vacations or holiday time. When we found his social media page, we noticed that he would post being at a bar or party on days when he'd called in sick.

We continued to watch his posts for a couple more months; each time, it was the same, and some of the posts involved him in lewd acts. He was not shy about what he posted. When we confronted him, he tried to tell us we had no right to look at his social media page because it was an invasion of his privacy, and he had the right to post whatever he wanted without fear of retaliation. He also claimed he had the right to call in sick without being questioned about any illness. He did have us there; however, one would think a police officer would know how the law works.

If your site is not locked to where people have to register or ask permission to see what you are doing, it's open for anybody to view, and the expectation of privacy is no longer valid. We located pictures of girls wearing nothing but his work shirt, with the patches and badge still on the shirt, letting everyone see what agency he worked for.

His actions were the cause of a new policy to be written about not posting anything involving the recognition of the agency, especially photos of someone else wearing a work shirt and nothing else. He was given a written reprimand for his behavior and had to sign the new policy—as we all did—acknowledging he understood the penalties if not followed. However, some people never learn and are victims of their own stupidity.

A month later, he called in sick. His social media site was reviewed again to see what he was up to. Again, he was out partying. This time, he wore his uniform, including his duty belt and weapon, at a Halloween party. While holding a bottle of whiskey, he faced a camera and flipped the bird. The caption for the picture was, "Fuck my job. I will do what I want when I want!" This ended his career in law enforcement, as he was immediately terminated.

If a proper background investigation had been completed, it would have been noticed before his being hired that he posted racial slurs and racist pictures on his page. It was also found that he had an active warrant for his arrest before being hired and was not caught until he applied for another agency that arrested him on this warrant. But wait—there's more! It wasn't just our agency that hired these fine, upstanding members of the law enforcement world.

An adjacent city we worked closely with had its share of hiring the criminal element, as well, because there was no background completed at all. Joshua was one of those officers. He was a firefighter for a short time but really wanted to be a police officer. His father worked at one of the state correctional facilities, and Joshua wanted the same type of career—except he wanted to work the road and not in a jail. After attending a police academy, he was hired on to the department in the adjacent town.

The town did not pay a lot, and officers would have to get second jobs to pay their bills. They were not put through proper field training and would often come to us to get help on cases or go through their yearly firearms training. Joshua had worked in this town for about a year when he decided to steal from one of the local businesses in our town.

Before being hired on to the department, he was a security officer at this business. One night, after the business was closed, he walked in through the back door. It was obvious he knew where all the cameras were, as he kept his baseball cap low and avoided showing his face.

He even walked past another employee who wasn't paying close attention. He walked straight into the area where a lot of cash was kept, without any hustle at all. He took over a hundred thousand dollars in cash and simply walked out the back door of the business. When the establishment opened the next morning, we got the report they had been burglarized of said amount of money.

We were able to obtain video surveillance of the incident. He committed this crime without a care in the world, not thinking he would ever get caught. However, some people are identified by how they walk and talk or even by specific clothes been seen wearing before. Joshua had a particular gait. Our detective had called a couple of us in to view the video, and we all agreed it looked like Joshua simply because of the way the suspect was walking. We could not prove who it was just by the gait, however. It was going to take way more than that.

After several months of the investigation, we thought we were at a dead end with the case. We had no evidence and no suspect, the only person the suspect had walked past hadn't been paying attention to who it was, and there were no further leads to go on. That is, until one day, we noticed Joshua was riding a brand new Harley Davidson motorcycle. We thought it was strange, as we knew how much money he made working in that department, and he had no other job. He was also driving a newer vehicle. His being able to afford these items wasn't adding up, especially since he'd previously told us he paid cash for everything.

A coworker of his then came by one day wearing a new duty belt and a new firearm. We knew it was new because he wanted to use our range to shoot some rounds through it, and we knew this kid could not afford these items, having a new baby and living off his normal salary. This was a case opener; we had an idea of who the suspect was, and now money was being spent on things we knew he couldn't afford. With a search warrant issued, we began looking into Joshua's financials. He was making $17,000 a year and paid outright for this motorcycle and truck.

The places where he'd bought these two items were contacted, and they confirmed that he'd paid cash. The purchase of the duty belt and gun for the other officer was found to have been purchased by Joshua with cash, as well. He had bought these items for his fellow officer using stolen money. Some of the cash could be recovered from these locations, allowing us to match the serial numbers to the stolen money. We now had our suspect, Joshua. After the case was finally brought to a close, he was found guilty of all charges, and sentencing was scheduled for a month later.

The day came for Joshua to appear in court for his sentencing of the burglary charges, and the judge wanted law enforcement present in case Joshua decided to get violent. Two other officers and I, along with two county deputies, were in the courtroom. The judge went over how disappointing it was to have to charge someone in law enforcement, and because of that, the maximum sentence was to be given.

He told Joshua nobody was above the law and that he, of all people, should have known better than to commit this type of crime and try to get away with it. It was also inconsiderate and unprofessional to buy another officer's equipment with stolen money, leaving that officer with nothing moving forward since those items were taken as evidence. We noticed Joshua was starting to cry, which the judge acknowledged by telling Joshua he should cry for the shame he had brought upon himself and his family.

The judge simply ripped into Joshua for about ten minutes before laying down the final sentence of fifteen years, the maximum time allowed. Following sentencing, it was revealed that Joshua would be serving his time where his dad was a correctional officer—the final nail in the coffin and the ultimate shame.

Joshua asked the judge if he could have a couple of extra weeks to get his affairs in order before starting his sentence. This made the judge laugh out loud, which I had never seen happen in this courtroom. The judge told Joshua, "You had plenty of time to get your affairs in order. You have fine minutes to say goodbye to your family, and you will be taken in custody immediately." There was a concern Joshua would try to escape the courtroom and run, but he didn't. He said goodbye to the family members who had shown up, and off he went to serve his time.

Promotion

I was promoted to sergeant with the department and ran a team of five officers. Now I was in charge of officers I had worked next to, spent off-duty time with, and gotten into trouble with, and I had to learn to separate that friendship from being their direct supervisor. This was difficult; I still wanted to be one of the guys, and at the same time, I would have to provide potentially bad evaluations, written reprimands, and terminations if instructed to do so by the command staff, whether I agreed with them or not. I was also responsible for dealing with complaints or investigating their inappropriate actions that occurred both on and off duty.

Before my promotion, the chief sat down with my wife to explain to her the responsibilities I would be taking on, including having to cover shifts if needed, working late on cases when a supervisor was needed, and any other assigned tasks provided, such as attending city council meetings on certain occasions. He wanted to ensure this would not cause an issue with my family. This department was small enough that everyone was part of the process, including our family members.

Separating friendship from work was a quick lesson for me when one of the officers I had known and worked closely with for several years became an issue within the department. It was made even more difficult because my family had had him over for dinner. We regularly hung out on our days off. He was like an uncle to my youngest daughter. His issue was not excessive force; it was straight-up constant insubordination. He refused to take cases or follow orders if he didn't think it was his job or if he believed the case was too petty and beneath him. If something didn't come from his direct supervisor, he would flat-out refuse to do the task, advising that I was not his supervisor and that if she agreed, she could tell him to do it.

He would yell down the hallway such things as "Fuck this department," "All they want to do is screw with everyone," and "I will not take bullshit cases; give me cases I want, not just because." Keep in mind this is a small town, and we didn't have a lot of major, big city-type cases—still, the cases we did have needed to be investigated by those who worked the day shift and could spend the time tracking down victims and witnesses. It wasn't as easy for someone was working graveyards; victims and witnesses did not like being contacted in the middle of the night.

Day shift officers had their own cases and assignments to complete. Adding more work would cause them to fall behind on what they needed to focus on. Since he was a detective, he would be assigned felony cases and some misdemeanors like sex assaults—cases patrol would initially get called to and then have to turn over because of the extent of investigation needed or the shift they worked. You can piss off witnesses easily by knocking on their doors in the middle of the night, so these cases were sent to the detectives for follow-up.

He would still attempt to make officers come in early or stay late because he felt these cases were beneath him. He would tell the graveyard officers they could work a few extra hours to follow up on their own cases. He saw himself as being in a position of superiority over patrol and had no problem telling the patrol officers he outranked them. I would learn about these issues when I would come into work and find a graveyard officer still working because he thought he needed to investigate the case himself; he had been told to do so by the detective.

This detective received a couple of written reprimands for his actions and his attitude toward me. After my promotion, I was tasked with looking at further disciplinary actions against him. I was looking into the abuse of authority toward fellow coworkers, issues of insubordination, and unprofessionalism while on duty. His direct supervisor was not asked to investigate these issues, as she had a tendency to side with his attitude toward investigating cases, and the insubordination and unprofessional conduct was due to the investigation of a suicide involving a previous employee.

After a couple of weeks of reviewing his personnel files and cases, it was determined he was not going to change his actions for the better of the department or himself. He wrote good reports, and the investigations he did complete were thorough. It was the insubordination that was getting him into trouble. There had also been numerous complaints from other officers and dispatchers that his actions were becoming concerning. There was concern he was going to become violent with some of the dispatchers—one, in particular, whom he had dated earlier on.

After this review, it was my recommendation to have him terminated. The written reprimands and suspensions just weren't cutting it; he wasn't learning. This was the most difficult decision I had to make in my career; he had been a friend at one time, and it truly sucked. However, I had a job to do, and I couldn't allow a friendship to get in the way of the stripes on my arm. So, I sent my recommendation to the chief, who in turn decided to keep this detective onboard even after all his transgressions.

The chief did inform the detective it was his recommendation to terminate, and his mind was changed by the sergeants. The chief was taking on the blame for maintaining peace and order among the ranks. This set the detective off even more, thinking the chief was out to get him. He believed this for a long time, holding a deep grudge against the chief, who'd actually stuck up for him. The detective didn't learn the truth until long after he'd left the department—that I and another sergeant had recommended the termination, not the chief. It didn't change how the detective felt about the chief. I learned some officers don't take responsibility for their own actions. They have to live their lives placing blame on others for the way they act.

Even as a sergeant, I was taking calls for service and completing my own cases. I also learned being a sergeant for a small agency was not always the best job. There were times when I would have to cover shifts due to illness, meaning I worked thirty-six hours straight on a few occasions. This is not really good for the body. By the time I completed these shifts, I was exhausted and irritable. The drive home seemed to take forever. It was also a very political position. The rank of sergeant was directly below the chief, so there were times when we would have to attend city functions on his behalf or attend council meetings to get funding for new equipment.

Other than that, it was still a good job to have. I was in charge of my team, made final decisions on certain things like equipment and case filings, and trained several officers coming into the department. I was also the field training coordinator; I was in charge of all new trainees and the training officers, along with training revisions if needed. The one big difference between being a patrol officer and a sergeant was that I was called in to help with cases when off duty. There were times I would get called in the middle of the night because of high-risk incidents, deaths, or cases that were too much for patrol officers to handle.

We responded to bomb threats called into the casinos or the school, along with my normal SWAT call-outs. Being a sergeant in the SWAT team also meant there were times when I was the team leader, if the original team leader was not available. I was never truly off duty. Often, I was the first one there and the last to leave. During the five years in this position, I learned there were a lot more stressors than at the line level, especially when the chief was not available. Sergeants had to step up and take command of the department and all actions relating to the department.

After twelve years of small-town fun, it was time for me to move on. I wanted more in my career than what the department could offer: a chance to move around and get out of patrol if I wanted, the ability to take more exciting calls, promotions ranking above sergeant, and, of course, more money. I had been contacted by other officers who had gone to larger agencies, telling me how awesome these larger departments were. So, I applied to one just to see what would happen, and several months later, I received an offer of employment. I had to tell my chief I was leaving the department for something bigger and better.

Much to my surprise, the chief was very supportive of my decision; he knew he wasn't able to offer me more money to stay, and the only other position above sergeant was his, and he wasn't ready to retire just yet. After working in this town for so long, I'd gotten to know several of the citizens and regulars who visited. It was a difficult choice to leave all that behind, as I enjoyed the people and the community for the most part, along with most of the people I worked with. After receiving the final job offer, I packed my office and said my goodbyes. I think the citizens I had known for so long took it worse than the rest of the department. It was hard to leave, but I knew it needed to be done.

Part V: A New Beginning

"A true police officer fights not because he hates what's in front of him, but because he loves who stands behind him."

—Unknown

Another Academy

When I started with my next department, I had to go through a short police academy to learn how the department worked, how paperwork was filled out and reported, what went to investigations and what didn't—and, of course, the city streets. This was my second academy in my career, and it was eye-opening to learn what patrol did and did not do.

I had to pay to go through my first academy. However, this time, I was hired by the department, and they placed me in their academy, where I got paid to learn the department's specific way of doing things, which was nice. I was the oldest in this academy and had the most experience. The instructors expected more from me because of this experience, especially when writing reports and knowing the state laws. At the same time, they were lenient on me because of my experience. By this time, I had been working the job for thirteen years. Most of the others in my academy had around five to seven years of experience, and some were from other states.

When responding to calls for service, I was used to investigating the cases from beginning to end. Now, I was in a department where cases were passed on to an actual investigation unit. My job was to get one call done; if it was not solved right away, I would send the case to detectives and move on to the next one. This was not an easy concept to get used to.

I enjoyed working on my own cases but also understood there would be more calls for service and no time to fully investigate the more complicated cases. Since we had officers from different states, it was interesting to learn what they did in their old departments. Some were used to writing and sending a report to investigations, and some would perform the investigations themselves. It was nice to get input from others on what needed to be placed into a report, and what details were not needed for the detectives.

This was another academy where we got plenty of exercise. There was time at the beginning of each day or the end for some type of physical activity, such as swimming, running, full-body circuit workouts, and playing sports like soccer. Every once in a while, our workout time would be during lunch. We would eat lunch in the classroom after the exercise program. I got into good shape during this academy and enjoyed the workouts provided by the academy staff. By the end of the academy, I did something I'd never thought I could accomplish: I ran six miles. It took some time, but I could run the whole distance, and I truly hate running.

The days of arrest control were painful, as we completed the training as if fighting in real life. It was good to train this way, but recovering would take a few days. Almost everyone received some injury during the training. I was placed on light duty requirements for about a week and rushed my recovery. My fear was not being able to finish the academy or being excused from the academy because I could not complete final testing. If this were to happen, I was not sure what I was going to do. My old department probably would not have hired me back, especially if I was injured and couldn't do the job right away. So, I fought hard to recover and keep my spot.

Part of the training was getting sprayed with pepper spray and hit by the Taser—the full five-second ride. To this day, I would still take a Taser ride over getting hit with pepper spray. The Taser is only five seconds of pain, and then it is over just as quickly. The effect of pepper spray can last anywhere from forty-five minutes to several hours. You can't take a warm shower to get the pepper spray off, as warm water reactivates it, and the burning can start all over again.

When it reactivates in the shower, it is no longer just on your face. This stuff does move down, and the burning may be in the genital area, which is a pretty uncomfortable feeling. We had a choice between getting hit with pepper spray or the Taser. We could have opted out of getting hit with either. But the old man in the group wasn't about to be shown up by a bunch of youngsters, even if he had been hit four times with a Taser in the past several years. I played along and took a hit from each one.

During Taser training, the instructors wanted to know if someone could feel it through a heavy bulletproof vest, so I volunteered to take the hit wearing the vest. After anticipating the hit with the probes, I heard the Taser go off and expected the pain to follow. But the darts did not penetrate the vest enough for me to feel any of it. Then, the instructors wanted to know if longer darts could be felt. This would help understand if a suspect could feel the Taser through a big puffy jacket. So, once again, I volunteered and waited for the Taser to be shot at me.

Anticipating that this time might hurt, I waited. After hearing the pop, I was relieved not to feel anything. The instructor told me that I had already gone twice. I did not have to take the ride without the vest, but when I looked over at all these young whippersnappers I was in class with, knowing how bad one of the recruits was getting harassed for refusing to take the ride, I told them I was ready and to "just do it." Third time is not the charm. The Taser worked, and I hit the ground like a ton of bricks. Damn, that shit hurts. But at least the others couldn't make fun of me for not taking it.

Having been doing the job for several years prior and starting over at a new, larger department was nerve-racking. There were concerns in my own mind that I would not make it past the academy. But I did. When the academy ended, I had to go through a short field training program, which put my knowledge of the streets and how calls were handled in order. I remember the feeling the first time I called for cover, and within seconds, I could hear the sirens blaring in the distance. Next thing I knew, several cars and officers were on the scene. I had never experienced this feeling. I remember thinking, "This is fucking cool." Help was just a few seconds away. At my previous department, there were plenty of times I would handle calls alone because the only other officer in town was transporting a prisoner to the jail— so I liked this aspect of the new job.

Field Training

My first field training officer let me do what I knew and was taught from my previous experience. As we arrived on calls, he would tell me he would just be considered a cover officer and wanted to see how I handled myself. After several calls within the first week, he reassured me I would do just fine.

We had a good time together as he continued to teach me the way of this department, trying to get me out of the old mindset from working in a smaller agency, such as letting a case go to investigations because I didn't have the time to work all my calls, especially the cases that were cold with no suspects and very little information. He also taught me which sergeants to trust and which ones shouldn't have been promoted in the first place.

During one shift in this first phase, we had to work with one of those sergeants the officers did not respect. This sergeant was not good at officer safety; nor did she know the laws properly. As we arrived at a call during one shift, this same sergeant pulled in behind us as a cover unit, even after being told by my training officer we didn't need a cover.

When we got to the call, I shut off the engine and started to get out of the vehicle.

As I opened the door, my training officer told me to stay in the car for a minute. Of course, I asked him why we weren't getting out. He just told me to wait a minute, and he would explain later. After we sat there for a minute or so, the sergeant decided she didn't want to wait any longer for us to get out. She then just pulled away and left the area. My training officer told me it was safe to get out of the car and explained that he did not want this sergeant on any scene, telling me further about her officer safety issues and lack of knowledge of the law. Working with this officer was a blast. It didn't even feel like I was in training most of the time.

Unfortunately, I had to switch training officers after four weeks and move on to the next stage with a new training officer. This one had me concerned after the first week. I felt like he was trying to wash me out. There was a large difference in how he and I handled calls, and an even larger personality conflict. He was black and white with everything; there was no room for discretion with this trainer. A ticket was issued if the law instructed to give someone a ticket.

There were no verbal warnings for speeders, verbal arguments, or whatever. Now, there are times when people need a ticket or must be arrested. But there are also times when a ticket does not need to be issued, and the person can be released, or a verbal warning can be issued because you can see the contact itself did the job. With this trainer, though—nope. If contact was made and a crime was committed, then a ticket was issued or an arrest made, and he wouldn't allow any other outcome.

Because I refused to follow his way of thinking, I kept getting low scores on my evaluations, and it was starting to concern me and piss me off at the same time— especially since he had been a cop for only five years longer than I had. He didn't have that much more experience than me. My biggest issue was that this training officer and the team sergeant were good friends, and I didn't think anything would be done about our differences, so I kept moving on, pretty much angry every day I had to train under him.

I was afraid if I said anything to the sergeant, I would be washed out for not getting along with coworkers or some shit like that. This guy was a douche, and he didn't give a damn who thought what about him. His job was to wash out officers; at least, that is what he continuously told me.

During the second week of training, I arrested a suspect we'd had to wrestle with to get him into handcuffs. This suspect did not want to go to jail. On the way there, my training officer told me to handle getting the prisoner into the jail as if I were working alone. He was not there to help me with anything, according to him.

So, I did as he said: I pretended my training officer was not with me and handled the transport into the jail alone. We had to park outside any secured area because the sally port, where we could pull our patrol vehicles for safety, was full of other cars. As I got the prisoner out of the car, I quickly glanced into the back seat area to ensure nothing was dropped.

As the suspect had already resisted once, I thought if I let go of the suspect to check the back seat completely, we may end up in a scuffle again, or the suspect might bolt. So, I just did a quick check. After I got the suspect into the jail and completed the booking process, I returned to my patrol vehicle and checked the back seat more thoroughly to ensure nothing was shoved down beneath the seat. Since I did this same thing when starting a shift and hadn't had anybody in the back seat today until now, I figured that if anything were found, it would be easy to pin it on the guy we'd just booked into the jail.

As we got into the patrol vehicle, my training officer advised me I would receive a low mark for not checking more thoroughly before taking the prisoner inside. I told him that since he'd wanted me to do things as if I were alone, it wouldn't have been safe for me to complete that deep of a search with the prisoner standing right there. He then told me it didn't matter if it would've been unsafe; that was how it needed to be done, and his way was the only way as far as he was concerned. This was the kind of shit I had to put up with for four weeks.

After some weeks into this second phase, his sergeant wanted to meet with me. Given the scores I was receiving from my trainer, I was even more concerned than I normally would have been. When the sergeant asked how I thought things were going, I flat-out told him I didn't feel comfortable saying anything because of how close the two of them were as friends. The sergeant advised me that their friendship had nothing to do with what was happening on the job. If there was an issue, I needed to speak up so things could get cleared up. Trusting what the sergeant was telling me, I spoke my piece about how much I thought the scores I was getting were bullshit and that my training officer needed to take into consideration that I was no rookie cop. The sergeant did listen to my concerns. However, he couldn't do much about my trainer because I could not be assigned to another. I just needed to roll with it, and I would be fine. The sergeant thought I was doing a good job, and he said I had nothing to worry about, so I did just roll with it.

Every day, my training officer and I would argue about something stupid, and he would mark me low in the section of getting along with coworkers. My training officer would constantly talk about his poker parties and who would show up, like I was supposed to be impressed or something. In the same conversation, he would remind me I was not one he would ever invite and not to expect us to be friends after this training. I am guessing his sergeant told him about my complaints, which didn't make him happy. I always kept thinking, *What an idiot.*

I'm not sure what type of people he hung out with, but if they were anything like him, I would rather punch myself in the face anyway than sit at a poker party with such a bunch of dipshits. After four weeks, I got away from this training officer and returned to my first training officer to get the rest of the training done and out of the way. I was released from field training and on my own right before Christmas.

Once on my own, I learned the differences between working under certain sergeants. Going from a small department to a large department, you didn't have a choice of what sergeant you got your first year. For my first-year bid, I was the last officer on the list and didn't even have to make the trip to choose my shift or sergeant. Since only one spot was left, I just had to call and find out where I was going.

For some, this may have been stressful, not knowing what they might get, but with my previous years of experience, I already knew I would most likely end up on the graveyard shift with some sergeant not liked by others. The good thing was I ended up on a shift with several of the officers I'd attended the academy with, so it wasn't like I was working with a team I didn't know. Being the last to bid, I had to work the southern end of the city called District Three, which wasn't so bad. They had fewer calls for service and were mostly considered the higher economic class of people.

The worst part was that I got put under a sergeant who was a complete tool. He was known to throw temper tantrums like a child and enjoyed micromanaging his team. He wanted to know what we were doing at all times and why we were doing whatever we were working on. As I said earlier, this part of the city was made up of a higher socioeconomic class of people. It also had some gang activity and action, though, the further north you went.

This was also where the lazy officers would bid, including the graveyard shift, so that they could go and hide. It was easy for them to do because it was big enough, and they would patrol their areas where little to no crime would occur—or at least say they were patrolling. Many would go and sleep in certain areas, making it difficult to find them.

Out of Training and On My Own

My first full year consisted of my sergeant not speaking to me several times because he would get mad at me for one reason or another. That's right; I said he would not speak to me or anyone he was mad at. He would give you the silent treatment for anywhere from a week to several weeks, depending on how much you'd irritated him. He would walk into a room and refuse to acknowledge your presence if he was mad at you, looking at everyone else but you. Specifically, he would walk into a briefing and say, "Hello, Bob," Hello, John," "Hello, Carla," etc. He would invite others from your team to coffee or dinner and never say anything to you. It was like a game with a pissed-off girlfriend. But hey, this was a fun game. How many times can you get the sergeant to not speak to you, pissing him off just to the point he couldn't do anything to you but that?

He was notorious for making traffic stops on drunk drivers. He would have the driver blow into a PBT, a small Intoxilyzer-type machine to measure breath alcohol content. He would then call someone over to complete roadside maneuvers and not tell the officer he already had an idea of the PBT results. The problem was that this was not a good form of measurement to use prior to conducting roadside maneuvers and was the cause of my getting my ass chewed in court twice. After the second ass-chewing by the District Attorney's office, I refused to complete the roadsides if I knew he had used this device. He would try to order me to do roadsides and get pissed if I refused those orders, threatening to contact the lieutenant to get their opinion. He couldn't get me for insubordination because he was trying to get me to do something against the courts. So, he would stop talking to me for the rest of the rotation.

There were several times this would happen during the year. I think he didn't like that I had more experience than he did and had no problem hinting at this fact. However, he did invite me to his Christmas party at the end of the year. Either he felt obligated, or I was supposed to feel honored; I'm not quite sure which it was.

This area was a good place to work during my first year out with a large department. There were good calls for service, and it was a slow-to-medium pace but enough to keep the night going fast. Of course, working the graveyard shift, the calls would slow down around three in the morning. I was still taking college courses for another degree while working this shift, so the downtime was spent parked in a church parking lot, completing homework assignments while watching the area for suspicious activity.

We also had some big calls: gang issues, suicides, a couple of vehicular assaults and homicides, and multiple verbal domestics, mainly due to money issues. Still being in the early stages of cell phones, before people started using them to record the police for everything, there was fun to be had. One particular family dispute involved two brothers fighting in the middle of the street about who would light the fireworks.

These were two adult men in their late twenties or early thirties acting like children at their mother's home. Of course, alcohol was involved. When I arrived on the scene, they stopped fighting while still hanging on to the Roman candle they were fighting about. As I approached these two, I immediately asked which one was dumb and which was dumber. To my complete amazement, the older one stated, "I guess I would be dumber." His reply caught me off-guard, but that was the type of people we dealt with in the middle of the night on the graveyard shift.

During this first year, half of the department's officers had to work the Democratic National Convention, leaving the other half of the department to work the remaining shifts. During this week-long convention, operating with a skeleton crew, there weren't many calls that ended up being too serious. The worst thing that happened was that a drunk driver killed a guy on a moped. The driver was a retired football player who had left the convention after having way too many drinks. On his way home from the convention, he was approaching a red light and didn't even begin to slow down or attempt to stop. I am unsure if he passed out or was simply preoccupied. As he approached the light, he crashed into the back of a guy on a moped who was stopped behind another vehicle.

The impact was hard, and the moped driver was killed immediately. There was brain matter in several locations, and the driver ran from the scene, so he was nowhere to be found. I did not recognize the victim's vehicle being a moped when I arrived on the scene. It had been hit so hard that it looked like an accordion. Since I was not the initial officer on the scene, I was directed to speak with a young female driver who'd witnessed the accident from beginning to end. She was very shaken up and unable to drive.

It took me several minutes to get her to calm down enough to talk to me. It was good she hadn't noticed a part of the victim's brain on the hood of her vehicle. I immediately got and kept her attention on me by standing slightly behind the driver's-side window and was able to talk her out of the car. Unfortunately, she did end up seeing the brain matter on her car when the crime scene investigators collected it, as they were not too slick at gathering that piece of evidence. Of course, she was trying to figure out why they were in her car. Due to the severity of the incident, several of us had to remain on scene for several hours after our shift ended.

If we hadn't, though, we might've missed the fire department running over part of the brains on the ground. Their truck became part of the crime scene; there was brain matter stuck to the tires that needed to be collected. They were pissed about having to leave the truck at the scene. Their chief kept responding to the scene, asking when their truck would be released. He was continuously told he could take the truck when the investigation was complete. This caused our chief to come to the scene and explain how a crime scene works to the fire chief. It was quite entertaining—tragic, but entertaining. After a while, the driver who'd caused the accident returned to the scene and explained he ran away because he wanted to call his lawyer for advice before turning himself in. Apparently, that is how rich football players react when they kill someone. All-in-all, the week wasn't too bad. It sounded like the officers that went to the DNC had more fun than we did: free coffee, free donuts, and a whole lot of sitting around.

During this first year, we did have some deaths caused by overdoses or that ended up being natural deaths. We didn't have to respond to any homicides in this district. We had some close calls, but the victims of stabbings or shootings survived. Robberies were common in the northern section of the district. We constantly ran on one of two different apartment complexes for these calls. One was a robbery of a Domino's in which the suspect left a trail of money leading right to his apartment. Besides the accident mentioned earlier, there weren't too many critical incidents that would have bothered me. The one I can recall was the death of a young child. It bothered me but was nothing I couldn't handle. It was ruled a SIDS death. The child apparently had rolled over and suffocated while the parents were sleeping. This was the first and only time I performed CPR on a child. The main issue was I had a little one myself—not young enough for this to happen, but still, concerning and too close to home.

One memorable call I had this first year was for a suicidal female. We were told the victim was trying to kill herself and had possibly taken some pills. When I arrived on the scene, I was directed to the garage where the female was currently located. Upon entering the garage, I noticed a female sitting on a bucket on the far side, wrapped in a blanket. Not being able to see her hands, I asked the female to show them to me so I'd know she did not have a weapon. After several times asking what was going on and seeing her hands, she finally stood up, opened the blanket, and presented herself stark naked. That's right—she wasn't wearing a stitch of clothing. She asked, "Do I look like I have a weapon?"

I immediately responded, "No, ma'am, you do not." After getting her some clothes, she told me she would only go to the hospital if I drove her. She needed to go for a mental health hold because she admitted she wanted to kill herself, but she didn't want to ride in an ambulance. Since I was the one who'd made contact and talked her down, she felt comfortable with me transporting her. On the way to the hospital, we talked about life and what she did for a living.

Come to find out, she was an exotic dancer and had lost her daughter in a court battle with her ex-boyfriend and his family. She then started talking about her boobs and how nice they were. She said, "You saw my tits; wouldn't you say they were nice tits?" I didn't want to respond to her question, as it was only her and me in the car, and I was working really hard at being a professional. I had heard horror stories of officers being accused of sexual harassment or assault, and I didn't want to become a statistic of this type of accusation. But she kept asking. Eventually, I agreed with her about her breasts, as I wanted the conversation to end. It kept her from asking again and stopped the conversation before we arrived at the hospital. It just goes to show that

248

you never know who you will come in contact with and how a situation will turn out.

After this first year, I moved to a district with more calls, but not so many we couldn't stay caught up. I didn't know it then, but this was the district I would finish my career in. There were plenty of different calls for service to make one a well-rounded officer, and I truly enjoyed this type of call volume and the different calls for service each night. The sergeants I worked under were all good to their teams and allowed their teams to do their jobs without thinking micro-management was necessary.

We responded to several homicides during my six years working in this district. Some were due to gang violence, and others were due to family violence. Domestic crimes were common, and some resulted in homicides. This district is where my experience was expanded even further. Learning how to work a homicide in a larger department taught me the different roles each officer has, not just one making all the decisions due to lack of manpower or not having a supervisor on duty at the time.

Detective response is also much quicker, along with coroner response time. It became clear that homicides were more brutal when they involved gang violence. It was like a spray-and-pray method: just pray you hit the person/people you mean to hit. Otherwise, anybody could become a victim of gang violence, from the elderly to infants. This is the kind of shit you hear stories about when working for a small department, never really expecting to respond to such an incident in your career. Small towns don't have gang problems to this extent; we only had the biker gangs come once a year to the town where I'd worked before, and they policed themselves.

There were a few I responded to on this larger department that bothered me later: loved ones crying and screaming over their child being shot to death, and other bangers showing up, trying to get in the way, yelling at the officers on the scene. The bodies would lie out in the open until the coroner arrived, allowing everybody and anybody to see the victims.

During the call, we would have to stay focused and keep moving forward, especially when other calls were pending. It was not like we could go back and debrief the situation or the response. We'd just keep working and put the incident in the back of our minds. Of course, if this stuff didn't get to you at least a little, there may be another issue going on that others should be aware of. You may be enjoying seeing dead bodies a little too much—or, in a professional opinion, there may be some form of psychosis present. The nights were busy enough to keep everyone moving and focused for each call, allowing us to rid our minds of the bad stuff.

Sexual Assaults

Sex assaults were a call everyone dreaded taking. Most officers were afraid to or simply did not want to take these calls and would avoid them like the plague. The calls were time-consuming and not exciting enough, tying up officers for hours with interviewing the victim and waiting at the hospital to collect the evidence from the rape exams. I took my share of sexual assault calls because I was still one of the newest officers, and it really didn't bother me.

I knew, somewhere down the road, I may end up helping a victim find their peace of mind and get an offender off the streets. I had to investigate many sexual assaults for my last department, and I had become efficient when working on these kinds of cases. Still, it becomes difficult when a victim is close to the same age as one of your own kids. That's a call nobody ever wants to respond to, but we had to take it and do the best we could, whether the victim was an adult or a juvenile.

Responding to these incidents can cause overwhelming concern for your own children, and you end up not wanting your own kids to hang out in places where they might be assaulted in such a manner. There is always the fear your child could become one of those victims, and it is terrifying. Out of all the sex assaults I responded to, there is one that always sticks in my mind. It was the last sex assault I had to take.

While on light duty one night, I had to work at the front desk. We would take phone calls and deal with people who walked into the front lobby to report crimes. Working at the front desk meant taking these calls and typing the cases before passing them on to patrol or investigations. A fifteen-year-old girl was brought in by her grandmother to report that the girl had been molested by her stepfather. The girl had been keeping a journal for seven years, writing about every time her stepfather sexually assaulted her.

The journal covered the first time to the last. I was told the girl would stay at her grandma's house often. Grandma had a designated room for the girl, so clothing and other items were always left at the house. When Grandma was cleaning the bedroom while the girl was in school, she came across the girl's diary. Not knowing what it was right away, Grandma started reading the journal. When she read about the assaults taking place, Grandma brought the girl in to report the assaults. The girl's mother had been confronted before they left for the police station, and she refused to believe any of the accusations. She also did not believe her husband was actually assaulting her daughter sexually and called the girl a liar. Therefore, Grandma sought help from the police on her own. Knowing the mother would take the stepdad's word over her own daughter's made my heart sink.

As I took the grandmother and girl into an interview room, I could tell the girl was not comfortable talking to me. She would not look at me nor look up from the table. She wouldn't even look at her grandmother. I was unsure if she was upset that Grandma had read the diary or if something else was happening there. As soon as we sat down, I started talking to the girl and asking her to tell me what was going on, but the only answer she gave was, "Nothing is going on. My mom doesn't believe me, so why would anyone else?" Grandma then handed me the journal and told me everything I needed to know was written down.

As I began reading the journal, I could see the girl had started it at an early age. She mentioned in one of the entries, "I am only seven years old. Why would he do this to me?" She then wrote down in detail how the stepfather would touch her in her "private area." He would then make her touch his "private parts" until "cream would come out." I skipped ahead a little. When the girl was around ten years old, he started having sexual intercourse with her.

She described this in detail, including how much it hurt and her just lying there waiting for him to get off her and leave her alone. I was getting sick to my stomach reading through this journal, wondering how in the hell a grown man could do this to a young girl and where her mother was while it was going on. After reading several of the entries, I told the girl that I knew it was not something comfortable to talk about, especially to me, but I did need to ask some questions.

What I learned during the interview was that her stepdad was the only person in the house who was working. Her mom didn't have to work, so she could stay home and take care of the house and the kids—that was what she was supposed to be doing, anyway. Stepdad had encouraged Mom to hang out with friends and join groups that would take her away from the home several nights a week. Having

Mom gone gave him time and opportunity to sexually assault this girl and the ability to deny it had ever happened if/when confronted. I was informed that Stepdad would tell the girl that if she said anything to anybody, not only would he deny it, but he would also make sure she never told anybody ever again. She did not specify what he meant, except to say that she believed he would seriously hurt her or make her disappear forever.

After the interview, Grandma took the girl to the hospital for an examination for evidence of sexual assault. I typed up my report and sent it to the sex crimes unit for further investigation. As I was on light duty, I was unable to work outside of the department. After I sent the report up to the detectives and knew who was investigating the case, I contacted the detective and asked if I could be in on the arrest when that time came. The detective allowed me to be there when this turd was arrested and booked.

When we arrived to make the arrest, the stepdad tried really hard to look like the best stepdad there ever was. Unfortunately for him, the case against him was overwhelming. The detectives had searched the house when he was not there, mainly the girl's bedroom, and found a lot of damaging evidence. As we took Stepdad out of the house in handcuffs, Mom was screaming, "That lying little bitch is just trying to get him in trouble! She hasn't liked him from the start!"

She kept going, stating, "Great, now I have to get a fucking job. He paid all my bills. He took care of me. It doesn't matter what he did. Now, I have to work because of that little bitch." Mom was later arrested for reckless endangerment by allowing the stepdad to be alone with the girl and placing her in danger without any concern, even after the girl told her the first time several years prior.

Since I was the officer who took the initial call, I was the only one called to court. The detective was on vacation, and they needed to keep going forward with the trial, so I was the one who had to fight for this little girl. Luckily, I knew the case from beginning to end and could testify on statements made and evidence collected. During the trial, the stepdad would talk about buying her whatever she wanted. Of course, we all know these were gifts for doing what he wanted with her.

Mom stuck to her story of the stepdad being innocent and then started getting upset because he would also be deported. She didn't know how she would pay her bills for the lifestyle she had become used to. The outcome of the case was that the stepdad would go to prison for a long time instead of being deported. Mom also had to do jail time herself because she'd left her daughter in this dangerous situation several times a week despite the child's attempts to tell her about the abuse. Reckless endangerment of a child was the final charge.

Unfortunately, the system does not work all the time. During my time with this department, I watched several sexual assault suspects walk away without any charges because the district attorneys didn't want to fight the case. They would dismiss the cases, citing insufficient evidence. If this didn't put a bad taste in your mouth about the court system, nothing would. Yet, as officers, we weren't allowed to give our opinions or thoughts. We just had to walk away and continue with the next case.

More Traffic Stops and Accidents

The number of tickets you were expected to write and how many drunk drivers the department wanted stopped depended on the shift you were working. Throughout my career, I hated running traffic. I would do everything possible not to make traffic stops. However, there were times when something would happen right in front of me and I had no choice. The drunk drivers I would pull over were never the ones I was looking for. I wasn't looking at all. They would just happen to be in the wrong place at the wrong time. Better yet, I was at the wrong place at the wrong time.

One night, while sitting at a stop sign and minding my own business, I noticed some crazy lady driving on the wrong side of the road. I remember thinking to myself as my shift was about to end. "Of course, this has to happen on my Friday at the end of my shift. Fucking people just can't behave." As I sat there watching from my stopped position, I really thought twice about making the stop. There were no other cars on the road. She had plenty of time to realize what she was doing.

Nobody would even know I'd seen anything. Then I thought, "Well shit, what if she hits somebody coming the other way? What if someone is watching me sit here and do nothing? Dammit, I'd better pull her over." With that in mind, I made the traffic stop so she didn't hurt anybody. As soon as I made contact with the driver, I knew she was so drunk she had no idea where she was. She actually thought she was in another city and was trying to figure out how she got there.

Apparently, she'd had a passenger at some point and was worried about where that passenger had gone. After I let her know why I was stopping her, she agreed to perform roadside maneuvers to determine her level of intoxication. She claimed to have only had three drinks. However, with the way she was stumbling outside the car and slurring her speech so badly—it was difficult to make out what she was saying at times—I was assuming she'd had way more than just a few drinks.

After having to stop the maneuvers for her safety, she was placed under arrest and transported to a detox facility, where she decided she wanted a breath test completed. To my amazement, she was barely over the legal limit of driving while intoxicated, at a 0.09. She was obviously unable to hold her alcohol. I had seen people in the 0.3 levels of intoxication with better control of themselves. This case went on to a Department of Revenue hearing to determine the suspension of her driver's license.

I absolutely hated these hearings. I would have to drive an hour and a half to the hearing, which lasted about fifteen to thirty minutes, only to drive back home and get a mere two hours of paid overtime. When this case went to the hearing, it didn't go as expected. I did not have to testify to the reasons for the contact and the lady not passing the roadside maneuvers, which was common practice. As soon as I entered the hearing room, she immediately started talking: "I know I was drunk when you pulled me over, and I know my license will be suspended. The only reason I requested this hearing was to thank you, in person, for pulling me over and charging me as you did with the DUI. I also want to apologize for my actions. This hearing does not need to continue any further. Here is my license."

I did not know whether to be pissed off over the time I'd lost in traveling all that way or to just be appreciative of her apology and her gratitude. I think I was more irritated, as she could have simply met with me at the police station and told me the same. We would have a long way to go before being able to complete these hearings via Zoom meeting like they do now.

Simple traffic violations were stopped and ticketed. I was to write so many traffic tickets a month. One of my favorite places to sit was near a No U-turn sign. I wasn't hiding anywhere. I was sitting in plain view where everyone and anyone could see me. From this location, I could write my monthly tickets in one shift. People would make U-turns at this location coming out of a grocery store parking lot instead of going out a different way.

There was not just one sign at this turn; there were two very hard-to-miss signs that clearly said no U-turns were allowed. It amazed me how easy it was to write so many tickets in such a short amount of time. Like I said, I didn't particularly appreciate running traffic. In fact, I hated it. However, according to expectations, I had to write them, and so I did. Of course, there were times when I could not bring myself to give someone a ticket.

One night, while running traffic at this favorite location of mine, I pulled over an elderly couple who were clearly from out of town. They were visiting one of their children and had decided they wanted chicken. The problem was that they got lost coming out of the parking lot, and the only way they could find their way out was to turn around at the no-U-turn intersection.

I made the traffic stop like I usually do, and when I approached the driver, I saw he was an elderly gentleman with his wife. The first thing he said was that he knew what he had done wrong. Then he told me he couldn't find any other way out of the parking lot and was trying to get the chicken back to the house before it got cold.

He and his wife were very friendly, offering me part of their dinner. The wife told me she had some paper plates and would be more than willing to put together a plate of food for me, which I respectfully declined. After speaking with them for a few minutes, I knew I would feel like an asshole if I wrote them a ticket, so I gave him a verbal warning and directions to get back to where he was going.

I would also run a laser once in a while to catch those speeders in other parts of the city. I gave a lot of verbal warnings unless someone started crying or gave me an attitude. The one I hated the most was the idiot asking, "Do you know who I am?" This was an automatic ticket because, for one, I didn't give a shit who they were, and for two, don't be an ass and expect to get out of a ticket just because of who you are or who you know. If you remember some of what I said when I told the story about stopping the mayor's son on Christmas night in the one-square-mile town, my follow-up response was normally, "I don't care if you are the son of God, Jesus Christ, you are speeding in my town, and even Jesus would get a ticket at this point." Of course, this sometimes led to a complaint being called in because I was being rude, but it was well worth it every time. I also knew my limitations of who not to give a ticket to.

One night, I pulled over a female in her twenties. As I made contact, I saw she was crying hysterically, which I assumed was because she was getting pulled over. Man, was I far off with that assumption! As soon as I contacted her, I asked why she was going so fast and if she was alright. The next thing that came out of her mouth was a vomit of her daily problems.

She had just found out she was pregnant, and her boyfriend had left her because of it. Her mom just kicked her out for getting pregnant, and if she was late to work one more time, she was going to lose her job. She was running late for that job because she was arguing with her mom. There were some other issues she had mentioned as well, but I can't remember all of them. These were just the highlights.

As a married man, I know when to step away and let things stand instead of making issues far worse than they already are. Okay—not always, but most of the time. This was one of those situations where I just decided to let it go, so I gave her a verbal warning and told her to slow down. I suggested she pull over into a parking lot someplace until she could get herself together a little bit and not cause an accident.

As I walked back to my patrol car, my cover officer immediately asked why I was letting her go with a warning. After telling him about the contact, he immediately said, "Oh yeah, you're married. Smart man." Either way, I always wrote the number of tickets each month. I thought it was funny that departments didn't like to use the word *quota*. Let's face it: we all know departments have one. They just like to call it "standards."

Of course, there were also traffic accidents—some more tragic than others, some more bloody than others. Not all included a victim being in another vehicle. Some were pedestrians struck by vehicles. We had a gentleman walking through his apartment complex parking lot one night, heading to his residence. A jeep that was cruising around the parking lot at the same time didn't see the pedestrian and ran him over. This was not your normal vehicle-versus-person accident, though.

When the jeep hit the guy, it rolled over the top of him, bending the guy in half. The jeep's driver immediately stopped, causing the other guy to be trapped under the vehicle with the hot exhaust sitting on the guy's back. When we arrived, I could hear the guy under the jeep yelling for help. I could also hear the fire department coming at the same time, but it sounded like they were still a good distance out.

While my sergeant was screaming over the radio to tell rescue to hurry up and launch flight for life, I decided to try and get the car lifted a little to relieve some of the weight and heat from the exhaust pipe off the poor dude under the car. I grabbed the jack from my patrol car and slid underneath. While talking to the victim and trying to keep him calm, I began jacking the car up.

I could only do one tire, as I had only one jack, and the sergeant was having a panic attack because of what I was doing. As soon as I got the jeep lifted enough, the firefighters and paramedics arrived on the scene and were able to pull the gentleman out from under the car. This poor guy was hurting badly. Besides having a car on top of him, he'd ended up with some bad burns on his back. But at least he'd survived.

At some point, I must have hit my head on something and cut it open a little. If you've ever had even the slightest of head wounds, you know they bleed like a running faucet. After we got the guy out from under the car and I crawled back out and was putting my jack away, several people asked if I was okay.

I kept saying I was fine. I could not figure out what the hell they were talking about; I'd seen worse accidents than this one. Finally, one of the paramedics told me to look in the side mirror of the ambulance. That was when I knew why I was being asked. I had blood all down the side of my face, and it looked like I'd opened a vein on my forehead.

Working in a bigger city with highways going through it means higher speeds and bigger, deadlier accidents. Most people drive fast and furious on the highways, not thinking about the outcome if they wreck their vehicle. One individual learned this lesson the hard way, flying around traffic and changing lanes at high speeds in his Cadillac Escalade. When he changed lanes for the last time, he clipped the front end of another SUV, which caused the back of the Cadillac to swerve out of control and eventually roll on the highway.

The vehicle came to rest across two lanes of traffic and upside down, lying on its top. Speeds were estimated to be more than ninety miles an hour in a sixty-five-mile-an-hour zone. Plenty of witnesses watched the accident happen and told us the driver of the Cadillac seemed to be rushing somewhere and driving recklessly. When I arrived at the scene, I noticed the driver was unconscious. I could not find a pulse. His color was changing fast. The EMTs arrived on the scene and confirmed he had died before their arrival.

As I looked in the back seat, I discovered two children in car seats—a boy of about five years old and a girl of about three years old. Both were okay, except for being upside down in their car seats and unable to get out. All I could think was to get them out before they realized their dad was dead in the seat in front of them. He hadn't been wearing a seatbelt, and that was more than likely why the crash had killed him. The firefighters were able to extract the children from the car, and we had to get them out of the area before their dad was extracted. Another officer got the kids back to the station and called their mom to come and get them. I could not imagine having to explain to these children that their own father put their lives in danger to get to wherever he was going in such a hurry. These situations are heartbreaking.

More Suicidal People

I was always grateful the situations I was in never escalated to a point where I had to shoot somebody. I shot plenty of suspects with the Taser, and one with the less-lethal shotgun with beanbag rounds. Hitting someone with a Taser was fun. I had been hit with this weapon four times during my career, so I knew how it felt. Deploying my Taser on a suspect while knowing of its effects made it better because I knew it was going to hurt like hell. My simple rule was if you ran from me and I got close enough to you, you were likely to be tased. I may not be a fast long-distance runner, but I was fast enough to catch up to someone in a short distance. Besides, as I've mentioned, I really hated running.

Of course, there were times someone was tased for their own safety rather than because they'd run from police or committed any crimes. I once responded to a welfare check on a man who had taken pills to try to kill himself. Luckily, his wife reported in the nick of time. When we were on scene, we could not see into the house because all the curtains in the front were closed. So, I started pounding on the front door to get the guy to answer it. As I was knocking, I heard a door on the side of the house close. I moved around to that side of the house, asking if anybody was there.

A six-foot fence separated me from the door I'd heard close. All of a sudden, I saw a hand come over the top of the fence. A man was looking up over the fence. I told him why we were there and that his wife was worried about him. While we were talking to him, he placed his other hand over the top of the fence while holding a large butcher knife in his hand. He became agitated immediately and told me to go away and let him do what he needed to. I asked what that was and what it had to do with the knife he was holding.

He said he just wanted to end his life and was going to kill himself in the backyard to make cleanup easier for everyone involved. I told him I simply could not let him harm himself and asked him to put the knife down and come out front to talk with us. In response, he yelled, "Get the fuck out of here and just let me die in peace!" He then ran deeper into his yard. I could still hear him yelling but couldn't make out what he was saying.

As my cover officer hid in the front of the house, I immediately found a way to the top of the fence. While straddling the fence, I unholstered my pistol and pointed it toward him. I was unsure if he was going to come after me with that knife, so I wanted to be ready to defend myself. I began talking to the guy and trying to convince him to put his knife down. I told him that killing himself wouldn't solve any problems for those involved in his life.

While talking to him, the suicidal man told us that all he wanted to do was put his dogs in the garage so that when we entered the backyard, the dogs wouldn't run out from the front entrance. I told him I would allow him to put his dogs in the garage, but he had to put the knife down; and if he tried to run into the garage himself, I would shoot him before he got the door closed.

After some back-and-forth, he agreed to put down the knife. He slowly walked to the garage and opened it, putting his dogs inside. I took the opportunity to holster my weapon and draw my Taser, as I didn't see any threat that required the use of deadly force. I just needed enough force to subdue him, put him in handcuffs, and place him on a mental health hold if needed.

As I was drawing my Taser, he turned and looked at me. He hollered, "Oh, hell no!" He grabbed the knife and began running deeper into the backyard. As soon as he grabbed the knife, I deployed my Taser and struck him in the pinky finger of his left hand and in the neck. He dropped like a rock immediately. The sergeant, who had arrived on the scene shortly after this all started, jumped over the fence to assist. My partner also finally made it into the backyard. She got the guy handcuffed.

After we got him secured and the medics placed him onto a gurney to transport him to the hospital, they began taking him out of the backyard. As we were walking out, he asked, "Are my dogs going to be okay?" I told him his wife was on her way home, which helped him remain calm. He then looked at me and said, "Officer, sorry it had to go this far. I'm just in a bad place. Thank you for not shooting me."

I looked down at him and told him our job was to make sure he was going to be okay and thanked him for not making me shoot him. He then said, "That thing you hit me with sure does hurt like hell, though," and chuckled. As I was leaving, I felt happy about how the call had turned out for him.

Of course, considering the city's size, we were conducting a welfare check on a possible suicidal party at least once a week. Even dealing with homeless individuals who were suicidal was common. Someone would call the police because they were concerned about someone sitting with a knife to their throat. Yes, we got a report of someone sitting on the side of a business holding a large knife to his throat while talking to himself and looking at a picture.

When we arrived on the scene, I grabbed my shotgun. It contained beanbag rounds meant not to kill, but only to injure and stop a threat without lethal force. When I exited my patrol vehicle, I racked a round into the chamber. The suicidal man said, "You know I will stab myself in the neck before that thing hits me." I told him, "I'm sure you would, but let's not try that theory." Another officer started to engage him and tried to talk him down.

This guy wanted to kill himself because his wife had taken their kids and left, leaving him in the city homeless and broke. He was holding a picture his little girl had drawn the last time he saw her, which had been several months. He truly believed he would rather be dead than have to fight for custody or let his daughter think he had just given up on her and his family. He was up and down with his emotions. The other officer was doing an excellent job of keeping him engaged, diverting his attention away from me. The distraction was needed, since he was still holding the knife. Several times, he would switch the knife from one hand and one side of his neck to the other.

After about twenty minutes of trying to talk this guy down, we were unsure of whether we could be successful and get him to put the knife down. Each time he got agitated, it was worse than the last time; he would calm down quicker, but he never took the knife away from his own throat. My sergeant advised me to take the shot the next time he changed the knife into his other hand.

A couple of minutes later, he had lowered the knife below his neck to swap hands and sides again. As he brought the knife down, I took the shot with the beanbag round and was able to get him to drop the knife. When he was placed into handcuffs, this guy was a mess. He was also a U.S. Army veteran dealing with personal demons, and it caused his wife to leave him out of fear. Luckily, we were able to get him transported to the hospital, where he could get further help.

Not all suicide cases we attended to resulted in lives saved. Unfortunately, some had already completed the task before we arrived. People would choose strange ways to kill themselves. Some would die slowly, and others would make it fast and painless. Some would attempt suicide without success, being in pain for several days before passing on. We responded to people who would overdose on what was called "whippits," where they would use a device to inhale the contents of CO_2 cartridges.

In most such cases, the number of cartridges it would take to end a life would be seven. Firearms are not always a definite thing, either. We responded to a male who had shot himself in the side of the head with a high-powered rifle. When we arrived on the scene, he was still breathing and trying to talk. His brain function was severely impaired, but his vitals were somehow still sustaining. He lived a little over a week before passing on. A sight one can't forget is that of a person with part of their head missing telling you telling you in a gurgling voice to leave and let them die. However, we do not comply with such requests. Our jobs are to save people's lives and not let them expire once we get on the scene.

A Close Call

As far as weapon use, it was not uncommon in this department to respond to calls where we had to draw our weapons during the shift. Drawing our weapons also depended on the situation: for example, when clearing a victim's home or business and dealing with hostile persons.

274

But every once in a while, we would get a call where intuition would tell me that we would have to take a life.

Some officers have never been in this type of situation, and some have had to take a life more than once. There were three times in my career when I thought I would have to shoot someone. However, one of those three times was the closest I had ever come. We responded to a domestic in progress with a weapon involved and observed by the reporting party. When we arrived on the scene, we contacted the suspect and victim. The problem was that the suspect would not listen to our commands. Our witness stated they had watched the suspect grab a gun from his vehicle and walk back into his apartment. They could hear people yelling from inside the apartment and were afraid someone was going to get shot. They even described the firearm he was carrying back into the residence. When we arrived on the scene, we could still hear the arguing from inside the apartment and immediately made entrance due to a reported firearm being involved.

I attempted several times to get his attention and make him turn around, but he would not stop yelling at his wife. He would first get really close to her, and then he would take a few steps back. His erratic actions made her put her hands up in a defensive motion, trying to shield herself from physical assault. Since he would not listen to our commands, I drew my weapon and pointed it at the suspect. His back was toward us, so we could not determine if he had the weapon on him or not. I continued to yell out very loud commands to him.

He would look back at us and then start in on his wife again, reaching for the front of his pants every time. At this point, we were thinking he was reaching for a weapon. I yelled one more time that if he didn't turn around and show me his hands, I was going to fucking shoot him. About this time, I began squeezing the trigger. I remember thinking to myself, *"Come on, asshole. Just turn around and show me your hands."*

He finally looked back at me. As I watched the expression on his face go from anger to fear, he immediately faced us and dropped to his knees on the floor, which I was thankful for. We didn't sign up for this job to shoot people. Police officers are supposed to protect the public, but I was also going to make sure the victim was protected.

While taking him to jail, we got to talking about the incident, and he told me the look on my face said I was about to pull the trigger and kill him. He wasn't the only person to say that who was on the call that night. My sergeant, who was on the outside of the house looking in through the back door. He also said the look on my face said I was about to shoot, and he was just moving out of the way.

Although I would have been justified in firing my weapon, I am glad I didn't have to. That call tired me out. When it was over, the adrenaline pumping through my body was so intense it just wore me down. I got many more calls like this one, and they would get me worked up to the point of exhaustion. The fatigue would be so debilitating that my hour-long drive home felt long and difficult. I would struggle to stay awake because the rush would be wearing off.

Not Worth Getting Worked Up

Even though my adrenaline would get pumping pretty well, I worked hard to maintain an outward calm. I did this to such an extent that, many times, I would be criticized for not getting more excited on the radio during in-progress calls. Now, some officers would scream on the radio every time they got excited, and you could not understand what they were saying. I was not like that; sometimes, dispatch would get mad at me for not sounding more excited.

I've always believed those who speak softly get more attention, even on the radio during a busy shift. The only times I would get excited on the radio was when others would not stop talking on the radio and the information needed to get out. Sometimes, people just talk to be talking because they think they are more important than they are. For the most part, whether it was a fight in progress, a fight I was involved in, or shots being fired, nothing worked me up to that point on the radio. My information always got out one way or another.

There was one night when shots were fired, and we had no idea where they came from, so other cars were called to my location to see if we could figure it out. This was a call at a party where there were several gang bangers, and we were there because of underage drinking. While trying to round up all these juveniles, someone had decided that firing a gun while the cops were there was a genius idea. Of course, we all started looking harder, as we had no idea if someone had been shot or not, and since we knew the difference between fireworks and gunshots, we knew someone was armed.

Anyway, when the shots were fired, I relayed to dispatch that I needed more cars to the scene; there were only

278

four patrol cars at the initial call. Because I hadn't sounded excited enough, the dispatch said, "Excuse me, did you just say shots were fired?" I calmly stated again that shots had been fired and I needed more cars to arrive at my location. This time, dispatch heard me, and several more cars showed up. After several hours of searching, we could not find where the gunshots came from or who'd fired them. So, we finished what we were there to do: write tickets for underage drinking.

Later that night, I was contacted by the sergeant on duty and advised dispatch was extremely upset with me for that call. I didn't know what he was talking about or what I had done wrong. I was told I was not excited enough about the shots being fired. I was told I needed to sound just a little more excited so dispatch knew they had to pay attention to what I was saying on the radio.

As I said, this was not the first or last time that dispatch needed to pay attention to what was being said. Instead of paying attention, dispatch got upset with me about not sounding more excited during calls. I know many officers the same way. Some people just never show excitement when shit hits the fan.

Don't get me wrong; I was amped up internally, and the blood was pumping—but since nobody could hear my excitement on the radio, it wasn't caught immediately. I just really never saw the point in screaming. Other officers tend to tune this out when it is a constant thing. We had officers who made everything sound like an emergency, no matter the call.

As I said, I was not the only officer with this problem with dispatch continuously. I had worked with a sergeant who was the same. He was also a shit magnet. Something would happen no matter what he was doing and where he was. One night, sitting in front of a department store after the store had closed, he decided to review officers' reports, since it was slow and nothing was happening. As he looked over these reports, he noticed two cars in the parking lot parked next to each other, with several people in each car.

After a few minutes, the parties in one car began shooting at the parties in the other car, who then returned fire. The sergeant immediately got on the radio and advised there were two cars involved in a shooting and that he needed more cars in the area. This caught me off-guard, as he didn't sound too worked up about the incident. Dispatch had to ask him to repeat his transmission, and he calmly said, "I need more cars in my area. There are two vehicles occupied and taking shots at each other while driving around in circles in the parking lot."

Holy shit! See? This guy couldn't go anywhere without something serious happening just out of the blue. By the time we got there, both vehicles were already gone. The sergeant and I were talking later that evening, and he told me he got his ass chewed because he made the incident sounds like it was no big deal. He told me, "They weren't shooting at me, so why get too excited about it?" I got the logic behind his way of thinking, but I did tell him we may have caught both cars if he'd sounded just slightly more excited. Thinking back, that was kind of ironic, as I was a big offender myself.

Deaths

One of the most horrific crime scenes I was called to was one that ended up being a mass shooting. Mass shootings are not uncommon these days and are happening more frequently. I was not on duty when the call came out, so I cannot take credit for being one of the responding officers. Several other officers were and did a damn good job on this call. I can say that because I heard the recordings of the radio traffic and the on-duty lieutenant in charge—who also did an outstanding job for this being the first time he had to handle such an event; he was cool-headed and calm. As I said, I was not on duty during the call.

However, due to being on the Emergency Response Team, I was called in after the incident happened. Unfortunately, I did not hear my phone ringing until several hours later; they were trying hard to get hold of anybody and everybody to respond as quickly as possible. Upon arrival at the department, I was placed on the scene for security while the crime scene investigators, detectives, and coroner completed their parts of the investigation. I was placed with one of the officers who had responded when the call came out and was part of transporting patients to nearby hospitals.

This officer was not in a good state of mind and should not have been placed with me at the location I was securing. He should not have been working at all, because of the effect it had on him and others who were still working or coming back to work. The location we were securing was the bloodiest corner of the building. All the injured victims had made their way out of the building from there, and this was also where the bodies inside were being brought out. You could still smell the blood on the ground, as it was still that fresh—a smell you can't ever forget. It kind of smelled like iron.

After he and I talked for quite some time, he had to use the restroom, which I convinced him to go to the station to do since we were not that far away. Once he left, my sergeant arrived at my location, asking where the other officer was. I told my sergeant he had need to use the restroom and I'd told him to go to the station. I then advised my sergeant to send this officer home as soon as possible because he was not in a good place mentally. I advised my sergeant this was not a good location for him to be in and that it was really messing with his mind to have to sit here.

Shortly after the officer arrived back at my location, he was called off and replaced with another officer who had not been on the original call. This was the extent of my exposure to this major critical incident. Talking with the officer placed with me initially just tore me up, seeing the pain in his eyes and how much the call had affected him as a person. Having to listen to what his role was in the incident made me hurt for all who did have to respond.

This call impacted many of the officers that night. It was never something an officer would think they'd have to deal with in their career, and yet it seems to be happening more and more often. Even though many of us were not directly involved, we were affected just by having to provide security at the scene. The sights and smells were horrendous and very strong.

The terrible thing was we had a few officers who took advantage of this case. They claimed to be on the scene and injured when they were never close to the scene. Apparently, they wanted to have some of the limelight surrounding the case and make sure injuries were covered and paid for by the department. They thought lying about how their injuries had happened was a good idea. Unfortunately, these types of officers are in several departments, which is shameful. But then again, individuals within every kind of business will use a terrible tragedy like this as an opportunity to make false, fraudulent claims.

When a department has the response of this one that night, it is easy for people to claim their presence, saying they were somewhere at the scene but unable to explain what they did. It was disturbing to know officers were transporting victims to the hospital because medical personnel would not respond to the victims for fear there may have been another shooter. I could not imagine the scene before I got there, and neither can many others, but we know it would not be something we'd want to see.

There was a lot more death in the city than there ever had been in my last department. You never knew what you would be called to during your shift. It could be slow and steady or just adrenaline-pumping calls all shift. More often than not, we didn't have time to sit down and eat dinner. When we could go to a restaurant and order a meal, most of the time, it would have to be boxed up for later, or we would just have to leave without ever seeing our food.

Because of this, I always had food with me. I never knew what the day would bring, and I would rather be safe than sorry and hungry. There were many times when I would be driving like a bat out of hell, operating the radio and computer with one hand, driving with the other, and eating a bite of something between all that. It did make the shift go by faster and keep things moving, but again, you had to find time to complete reports for all of it, as well.

Catching up on reports was more common on your last shift for the week. If you didn't want to stay late on your Friday, you would have to make yourself look busy so you received no more calls until you were caught up on reports.

It was easy since our Fridays were normally double-staffed; the scheduling worked out this way. It's funny that television makes our job look so glorious, having fun all the time and going from call to call. Yet, they never show the officer sitting around in the jail or hiding in their vehicle parked somewhere for hours typing up their week's reports. Rookies have a hard time grasping this concept when they decide to join a police department. As a result, they complain when it comes time to perform the task. In reality, when you have a busy week, you end up with a crap load of reports to write. Writing reports is never fun, but it's better than getting called in on your days off because you didn't complete them.

Injured

After so many years of working as a road officer, I always knew my luck had to run out eventually. I tried working on investigations a couple of times and even tried my hand at a specialized unit. I didn't like either one. The specialized unit might have been better if I could get a glimpse of doing something more than just sitting around and surfing the internet for hours because the officers already on that unit didn't really want to do anything.

Working the short stints with the investigations units was even worse. It was all the waiting around for people to call you back or for evidence to be processed so you could move forward with your cases. The waiting just bored the hell out of me, and it made me want to be out on the road. I was not one of those guys who wanted to get off the road and out of a patrol car. I enjoyed every minute of every day working patrol, no matter how good or bad the days were. No two days were the same, and you never knew what would happen on your shift.

I can't say I never got injured during my years on patrol, because we all did in one way or another. My injuries were never severe enough to require reporting them for workman's compensation, though. I would just limp it off, wait for my days off, and recover in that period. There were only two times I had to report an injury. The first time didn't even give me any downtime. I just kept going, defying doctors' orders and hiding whatever pain I had. The second time was the one that hit me hard enough that I ended up having to work light duty and have surgery.

Unlike television, injuries seldom occur while doing something cool or what would be considered cool, like jumping over a fence in pursuit of a suspect, getting into a car wreck during a vehicle pursuit, or something along those lines. No, it's usually something completely out of the blue while doing something lame, like slipping downstairs or falling while searching for evidence. Of course, some officers would file a claim every time they received a scratch or bent their pinky finger a little too far back. But it so happened it only took one call and one serious injury to end everything as far as my career was concerned.

It was the first call of the shift. I, along with other officers, got into an on-foot pursuit with some juvenile purse snatchers who tossed the purse and contents under a bridge. While en route to the call, I contacted the victim, who described the kids who snatched her purse and took off running. I immediately aired the description over the radio and was shortly notified the kids were located and running through a neighborhood. As I came on the scene, we gave a short chase and caught one of the kids, who decided to put up a good fight. He didn't want to get arrested again and did his best to ensure this didn't happen.

After a few minutes of struggling with this little turd, he was taken into custody and transported to the jail. I then looked for the purse and its belongings. A witness had told us they watched a kid tossing something over a bridge into a creek. While walking around on large boulders looking for these items, one of the boulders tipped, knocking me off my balance and causing me to fall. Of course, I tried to brace this fall by catching my weight with my right arm. I immediately knew something had gone wrong with this fall but assumed it would be fine like it always was.

Since this was my Friday, I figured I could take my days off to recover a little and get back to work in a few days. Unfortunately, this was not the case. As I continued working my shift, I could feel the pain shooting up my arm into my shoulder; but again, I had days off coming up and believed I would be fine. At the end of my shift and working a busy night, I was getting ready to contact dispatch for one last traffic stop. As I went to grab the radio mic, I realized I had no strength in my right hand. I couldn't even squeeze the button on the mic. I knew this issue was more extensive, and I didn't see it ending well.

I used my fist to push the button on the mic to call the sergeant on duty and have him meet me at the station, just in case this issue didn't go away. This was my first and only serious on-duty injury. I'd had injuries before that had forced me into light duty, but those were all from doing stupid shit on my days off. After reporting it to the sergeant,

I was told I was pretty much being a puss and making the sergeant do more paperwork than he wanted to do. It was a burden to him.

The sergeant told me I had to make an appointment with the workman's comp doctor, since he had to complete a report on the injury. At the same time, he told me he had never been hurt on the job in his whole career, which I called bullshit on at the time.

Of course, I was placed on light duty after visiting the doctor and being told about the damage. I did end up receiving shoulder surgery and a damaged forearm that couldn't be fixed. Anyway, my time on light duty was eye-opening. I had spent many years working closely with several officers and heard them talk about brotherhood and watching out for one another. However, during this time, I learned all this talk was a bunch of shit.

During the year I spent on light duty, even when I was told by a specialist I would never be released back to full duty, I spoke to very few of those same guys. I tried reaching out to most of them and would show up to briefings to greet them. I never heard back from most of them. I even heard that these same officers believed I was faking the injury to get a retirement. Brotherhood, my ass! If they only knew how hard I tried to get back on the road. Talk about leaving someone with a feeling of loneliness. I ended up with very few I could call friends, and I still talk to them today.

After more than a year on light duty, I was retired from police work, never having the ability to do the job again. All those years of minor, unreported injuries, and the one injury I felt the need to report ended up retiring me. At some point, I just had to face the fact that my career was over. It was difficult to think I would never be able to go back on the road. I had both good and bad days. Some days put me in a deep depression, which was hidden from many others. I took my retirement and completed my career as a police officer, which was awesome, fun, and honorable.

Part VI: The Change

"The wicked flee when no man pursueth, but the righteous
are bold as a lion."

—Proverbs 28:1

You Don't Come Out the Same as When You Went In

Not everyone wants to admit they have changed during their career, and some won't even acknowledge a change in their personality. But many recognize the trauma they have seen and gone through themselves. Those who refuse to acknowledge that difference in attitude, anger, depression, mistrust, and anxiety are what I consider "self-stupid."

They are not stupid in what they know. They are stupid because they refuse to recognize who they have truly become. We are not the ignorant youngsters we once were before entering this work. There have been things nobody else wants to know about because of fear, yet we have faced that fear and dealt with those things that scare the regular person. There have been so many who have done this job for twenty, thirty, and even forty years.

Everyone has or had their reasons for wanting to get into law enforcement or be some kind of first responder (this applies not only to the police professionals, but also fire and rescue). I wanted to be like all those cops in the TV shows. I wanted to live the stories I heard growing up from the officers I knew in my hometown, including those from when I was dating the daughter of a local police chief.

None of them ever talked about the bad calls they responded to or the traumatic calls they saw or had to deal with. In the television shows, you would watch them respond to calls, kick some ass, and go back to work. You never saw the impact of getting involved in a shooting or them needing to step away for a few minutes because the crime scene was that upsetting or traumatic. All those officers simply went back to work, laughing and joking, responding to the next call like nothing in the world bothered them.

When I first started, all I knew was that I had to be twenty-one years old and have a somewhat clean record (i.e., not commit any crimes after eighteen, as these become part of a person's permanent criminal record). Besides underage drinking between eighteen and twenty-one, I made sure to keep my nose clean. Everyone I knew understood what I wanted to be when I grew up. One of my favorite places to hang out and drink was a known biker bar, *Sons of Silence*.

Getting to know these bikers was interesting, and they told great stories; yet everything they talked about made them look like angels. They talked about the good stuff they were into. They never tried to recruit me. I made it very clear I wanted to be a cop, and they respected or appeared to respect that idea. Looking back, they probably thought they would have great insight from someone inside the department, someone they could get information from when needed.

Before I started the academy, I moved out of the town and lost touch with all of them, which was for the best. Shortly after I left, I learned several had been arrested for RICO violations, Racketeering Influenced and Corrupt Organization Act. One even killed a college student at the bar, causing it to be shut down permanently. It's a crazy world out there!

When some people get into police work, they may have prior experience, good and bad—a history of drugs, theft, or other criminal background as a juvenile, for example—that helps them specialize in certain areas. Some of the best narcotics officers I ever met had a background consisting of extensive drug use. They knew how to talk the lingo and act around dealers and users, which made them good at their job. When I started, I wanted to know more about biker gangs. Hanging out with them and learning about their lifestyle and who they were intrigued me. I also had my way of catching other criminals, such as thieves and juvenile offenders. I was no angel growing up and knew what to look for.

Unfortunately, as I learned, the real world is not like that, as so many of us learned once we started working the job. Some end up dealing with this trauma nearly every day, and some several times a month. There are areas where death, trauma, and high-stress incidents happen nearly every shift worked. I read an article once that said a twenty-year officer who works patrol their whole career will face more than 800 critical incidents.

When I read that, I had to think hard as to what was truly considered a critical incident. I'm not saying I could recall *that* many, but compared to the average person who may face a critical incident a couple of times in their life, a police officer faces more. We frequently deal with dead bodies, serious or fatal car accidents, and shootings. It's safe to say that all these extreme situations add up quickly for many during their time on the road. Some officers will never have to deal with any of these situations, and they will go through their whole career never pulling their weapon or dealing with anything more than a domestic assault every now and then. Perhaps their most common calls will be thefts or other minor crimes. Every now and then, they might have to respond to a natural death or a suicide. But that does not mean they won't be affected by those calls.

Responding to serious calls all the time changes people. Whether it is recognized or not, we all are affected in some way. These changes can't always be explained. We try to think about the call that affected us the most and remember how we were before taking on such a job. When starting this career, it was because it is what we wanted to do, whether knowing as a kid from growing up watching our favorite police shows or figuring it out much later in life.

Some individuals may have considered being a police officer a job to pay the bills. They thought joining the police force would be interesting because television makes police work look so awesome—go to work, arrest bad people, get into gun fights, holster up, and continue with your day. Some even wanted to follow in a family member's or close friend's footsteps. The stories they would tell sounded exciting and honorable, definitely far different from a simple desk job.

Through all the great stories and conversations, the job stressors were never discussed, and I never saw any of my mentors grieve in front of me. I can't remember an instance when one of the officers I knew complained about working different shifts, working late due to a late call for service, or catching up on paperwork. They never talked about the infant who had died or having to give CPR to someone until rescue arrived on the scene.

I never heard about how you would feel at a homicide scene—only how to investigate that scene. The officers always described their job as the best job they ever had. They didn't have to worry about the sergeant attending all their calls, and they told stories of the funny stuff that happened. However, all that changed once the job started, and the more serious calls started to appear—the homicides, suicides, domestics, and so on. Then there are the constant changes in hours, not knowing what shift you have to work from one year to the next.

As soon as your system would get used to working graveyards and sleeping during the day, it would have to switch again. You would have to get used to that new shift, and the shifts where you would have to stay an extra four hours, knowing you must be back to work in eleven hours instead of sixteen. You may get to see your family, or you may not. You would have to cancel plans or vacations because you got subpoenaed to court or because of a shortage of manpower.

There was no training that could prepare you for what you were about to face in your upcoming career. This was mainly because the truth would scare many away. I even think about the media coverage happening currently or the easy use of social media. People do not want to do the job anymore because of all the bad publicity. Those who began this career path twenty or more years ago didn't have to worry about such things as social media. By the time any news channel got hold of a story, it was several days after the event and pretty much over. Now, many stressful issues happen daily, for the world to see, and seem to be added to all the time.

As I mentioned earlier, my first year was a learning experience. The most stressful part was learning how to deal with different people and ensuring my reports were completed before I went home. That was true up until a coworker was killed in the line of duty. This incident was a big changing point for me. Not only did I not quite know how to react, but it was kind of a shock to the system.

I grew up believing men don't show their feelings and have to be strong. I saw the hurt on the faces of many deputies—those I was close to and friends with. I knew the deputy who was killed; he was a friend to many, both on and off the job; but some had known him longer than I had, so I felt I needed to be the strong one for them, someone they could talk to. I felt I needed to be a shoulder they could cry on.

For some reason, I didn't feel I had the right to be upset. What I did know is I was not sure I could continue on this career path. It scared the hell out of me and made me think about my own family and what they would go through if it happened to me. After a long night of no sleep, I decided to continue, and I decided nothing would break me from completing my dream of being in law enforcement. In fact, this realization made me want to do the job even more, to do what I could to keep this from happening again in the future, wherever I might work. Unfortunately, some did not feel the same and got out of the profession altogether.

For so long, I put the loss of this deputy in the back of my mind and didn't take the time to grieve over the loss of him. I thought I had to move past it quickly because it was just part of the job. I'd been taught that in the academy. I was there for the other deputies, making sure to listen to them and help them through the situation, covering shifts when needed. I remember attending a debrief session where the therapist heading the debrief wanted us to open up and share our feelings and thoughts. The session became awkward fast when nobody would say anything, and the therapist ended up doing all the talking.

The funeral was an eye-opening experience, too. The amount of support from other agencies was impressive, to say the least. This was also the last time I could hear "Taps" playing without shedding a tear. Unfortunately, like so many others, there were more funerals to attend throughout my career, and the memory of this one would come back every time. I just didn't realize how much it would affect me personally and professionally in the years to come. You can attend all the training courses in the world where you are told how you might react and what you should do. However, until it happens, that training is just a bunch of talk.

As time passed and I moved on to my next department, my personal relationships took a hit. I grew distant from my friends outside of law enforcement. I even grew distant from my own family. I was often told that I was changing and wasn't the person I'd been before becoming a cop. There were several friends I had before whom I lost contact with once I joined the police academy. I tried to stay in contact but never heard back from them. It was like they didn't approve of my profession and wanted to distance themselves so they wouldn't feel uncomfortable; at least, that's what it felt like to me.

I had made many new friends who were part of the law enforcement realm, but I still refused to get too close. I had it in my head that if I kept my distance and if anything were to happen to me, it wouldn't hurt those around me so badly. This included my own family. I know it wasn't the right way to think, but it made me feel better about why I didn't want to get to know so many people. I met many others later with the same thought process, but again, not all would admit to it. I quickly began not trusting those I didn't know; I was becoming more and more antisocial.

I didn't want to be around people. I preferred being left alone and doing things alone without others getting involved. These changes went on for several years following Ken's homicide, and the longer I went without admitting to myself something was off, the worse I got with not wanting to be around people. I would only trust those who wore the uniform or wore a badge, and even that was stretching it.

Everyone else's intentions toward me or reasons for wanting to know me better were questionable. I lived, breathed, and bled the job; it was the only thing I wanted. Both on and off duty, I was always looking for and trying to spot the turds that surrounded me. If I wasn't with those I chose to be close to, including family members, I would do things independently outside the job.

My temper was growing shorter, even with petty stuff. I would especially get angry with officers who were unsafe and did reckless things, placing others' lives or their own lives in jeopardy. I understand that everyone gets angry, but I was angry to the point of going over the edge and yelling at officers in public without caring what I said. I would start arguments with those in my personal life just to have an excuse to leave and not be around them. I didn't want to attend another cop's funeral, and by this time in my life, I had been to about four funerals for those I knew personally and for several others to represent a department presence.

Any time someone would point out my short temper or how much I had changed for the worse, I would get angrier at them and end up in an argument, telling them they didn't know me as well as they thought they did. In my mind, they were the ones who were different and acting differently toward me. I was still the same person I always was, and nobody would tell me otherwise—not my friends, family, coworkers, or supervisors. Everybody else was wrong, and they just needed to leave me alone.

The one thing I didn't get into was drinking much alcohol. I would not allow myself to get to this place. I was part of a SWAT team and needed to make sure I was sober at all times in case of any call-outs. I didn't want anything to alter my mental state. I was always ready, always alert. I was hyper-vigilant. I buried myself deeper into my job, ready for anything at any given time. I always wanted to be ready for SWAT call-outs or coverage of other shifts when needed. I also came from a family history of alcoholism and wanted to make sure I didn't follow that path.

Even though I didn't like attending the funerals (of course I didn't—who would?), I would still show up. I could hold my feelings together until "Taps" played, and even though I may not have known the officer, this would always cause my emotions to show. Many will know what I am talking about—not just police officers, but also first responders and military personnel. Of those four officers I knew who died, all had committed suicide. Nobody ever saw it coming. They hid their issues very well and would not talk to anybody about what was bothering them, not even their families. When asked, they would just say they were doing all right and immediately drop or change the subject.

As they hid their problems, their depression would grow deeper and harder to climb out of, and their problems would get bigger. Some would drink themselves to sleep every night. They were also likely to be in financial debt and go through a divorce. They further had issues within the department, from use of force issues to straight-up making bad decisions within arrests, paperwork, and policy violations. But this was also a time when not much was talked about when it came to officer suicides. The ghosts taken home at night could be dismissed and put into that little box in the back of your head where, eventually, they were hoped to disappear and never return.

The worry was that if the ghosts *did* return, an officer would have to hide their feelings due to fear of being called weak and taken off the road. They would have their gun taken for safekeeping and be made to drive a desk until it was determined they were not going to injure themselves or anyone else. Hence, emotions resulting from extreme situations were considered weaknesses that needed to be concealed.

While working in this department, I realized how severe the situation regarding suicides among first responders is. The issue was quite frightening, and so was the fact that no one was willing to talk about it. It was never really stated how many officers would take their own lives coming from other departments. Departments were just quick to say officers passed from natural causes so as not to place blame on those who died in this unfortunate way. At the time, anger grew deep within me at the thought of officers committing such a cowardly act. I was angry about what I considered the selfishness of those taking their own lives, taking the easy way out, and leaving behind those close to them.

Now, don't get me wrong. There were a couple of times when I was at my lowest and wondered if anybody would even miss me if I drove my car off the side of a mountain or into a post. This didn't happen, but the thought had crossed my mind several times. As mentioned earlier, in my mind, they should have just been able to put their issues in that box in the back of their mind and continue on with their life, not end it.

One thing I noticed was that first responders, mainly police officers, did not show the usual signs of suicidal thoughts. They wouldn't segregate themselves or give away belongings; nor did they leave notes for others to find. The reality was that they knew what they wanted and did not want to be stopped. They will have been to calls where there were signs of suicidal ideation, and preplanning was not in their thoughts. Having the experience of responding to these calls, they knew what signs not to leave behind, even to the point of agreeing to meet with a friend later, knowing they would not be alive for that meeting.

One officer did exactly that; he was having a bad night, and when the shift ended, he went home. The sergeant called to check on him and make sure he would be okay and wanted to know if anybody could do anything. The officer stated he would be fine. The sergeant told him to call when he woke up, and they would go have coffee, which was agreed upon.

Immediately after the officer hung up the phone, he took his own life. There were no warnings. There was no mention made to anybody. It was later found out that his wife had left him two days prior, and he thought he was getting fired from the department.

One thing I noticed about many of the people I worked with or met in law enforcement was that they had no problem putting down at least a six-pack of beer a night following a shift. Some even put down a lot more beer, or something harder, each night when they got home from work. The drinking would be more extreme when they'd have days off. Alcoholism runs high among police officers, and I witnessed this firsthand. Not all of it was due to the job, however. Some were having money or relationship issues, or both, and alcohol was a way to get out of their own head each night when they got home from work.

When I talk about getting out of their own head, they would drink until they passed out from intoxication, escaping reality. Of course, some would drink to get rid of the mental image they had from something that happened during their shift, like a homicide. Many would not acknowledge they had a problem and would say it was just a way for them to get to sleep, justification for consuming high amounts of alcohol.

However, they were at least able to deal with others outside of law enforcement, having the ability to be in crowds with a bit more comfort after a few drinks. I, on the other hand, had a big issue with being in crowds and didn't trust anybody outside my community of cops. I did not drink much. I would only indulge once every few weeks; even then, it was only two, maybe three beers at the most. Beers or not, crowds were very nerve-racking for me, as they are for many.

Statistics have shown that both alcoholism and divorce are high among police officers. A police officer's work carries a lot of stress, and they endure much pain and often hide it from those closest to them. They do not want to appear weak to their coworkers or leaders, and they can't exactly talk to their significant other or family about their day, as it would be too disturbing for most. So, they hide the pain and anger. While the issues are building inside, they are outwardly driving away those around them, including their own families, wives, and kids. The more these problems surface, the deeper they go into the bottle.

They consume more alcohol to get rid of the pain they are facing and the troubles they are having at home. They begin to have more issues at home; and interdepartmentally, job performance becomes a bigger issue. They lose sight of why they joined the department and begin to break the rules, trying to hide their actions because they know they're wrong. Eventually, the Internal

Investigations department starts to get busy investigating complaints brought by citizens.

Not all complaints are about officers having difficulty within the department. Many complaints come from citizens who are angry about being pulled over for a traffic violation, and the citizen thinks it is a waste of everyone's time since there are "more serious crimes to go and take care of." The real issue is when complaints come in consistently on the same officer for policy or law violation, such as rudeness, excessive force, traffic violations they've committed themselves, breaking the chain of command, covering up mistakes in arrests through their reports, falsifying reports, insubordination, and false testimony in court.

There are so many other issues to be talked about, but also too many to mention; these are just to name a few. Instead of seeking help outside the department, these actions worsen and become bigger with each infraction. Eventually, this can lead to termination from the job, making things worse for the officer in their personal lives. When an officer is terminated from one agency, the likelihood of getting another job in the law enforcement world is very slim, thus taking away the possibility of living their dream. Another consequence might be that they are criminally charged for a crime, committed either on or off duty. Then, they could get jail time, ending their career just as fast.

Suicide and alcoholism seem to be a way out for so many. However, it's not necessarily the job causing the climbing suicide rate or the excessive drinking; it's the aftermath of the stress from the job. I once had a conversation with a psychologist on this topic, and it made me wonder if this hypothesis was correct. I had to start looking into those I knew who had committed suicide in my time. I realized there were so many reasons for making this drastic choice, and those reasons go beyond the job itself. So, I have to agree that it's not the job that is the cause; the job is merely one factor alongside many others. What majorly contributes is the silence about things officers encounter on the job and their inability to talk or take the opportunity to talk to someone professionally.

So many officers turn to alcohol and substance abuse instead. They even have fits of rage, taking out their anger on those who are least deserving of it. I am speaking about spouses, children, friends, and other family members. Even members of the public who do nothing more than try and defend themselves verbally against accusations of a crime or are in the wrong place at the wrong time come under fire.

Everything seems to build up, placing the officer in a situation that seems too difficult to escape. To this officer, there is only one way out: ending all the pain for them and those around them.

However, these aren't the only issues causing an officer to take their own life. Some can't see themselves doing anything else but police work. When they commit a criminal act, like domestic violence, they know it will end their career. They don't want to live the rest of their life knowing what they did "ruined their life." They are also afraid of doing jail time—they are concerned about being placed with people they arrested and knowing facing the associated dangers; they believe the only way to avoid this outcome is to end their own life.

The fear of not doing the job anymore and not feeling like they are accomplishing something meaningful could be the reason for suicide right before or shortly after retirement. There is also the possibility of not being able to find that daily adrenaline rush we have during a shift. It's almost like they know nothing will give them the same rush, and so they feel useless. I have heard of several from the last few years who took their lives right before retirement after thirty-plus years of service, or within the year following their retirement.

I think this explanation is the only one that makes sense. Most men and women look forward to their retirement, not having to worry about working holidays, losing days off for training or court, and not dealing with the internal stress from the department. Yet, some can't seem to let go of that routine in their lives. Police officers don't know what is next for them during retirement, which can be scary. They think about what they will do when they wake up every morning, not having to wear that uniform, responding to calls, not knowing what is truly happening or how the call will end.

Every day is something different, and no two calls are the same; that is the most thrilling part about the job. Officers never know when something dangerous may come about. Yet, in retirement, it's the same thing every day; there is not enough imagination to think of things to do to maintain the mind's interest or give the same thrill. They don't want to travel because they still don't trust people or they're too aware of bad things happening in the world.

Hobbies are difficult to pick up because nothing besides being a cop interests them. Retirement sounds like a great idea for many; however, some can't let go of their job, and the thought of not doing the job scares the hell out of them. Without it, some retired police officers feel like they are nobody or nothing, so they go out on their own terms.

Some retire on their own after serving several years of working in law enforcement. They plan what comes next in life and may even move to a new area. Others are forced into retirement due to department cutbacks or medical issues. These medical issues could be due to an accident on the job, a mental or emotional difficulty, or simply getting to an age that makes it dangerous for them to work in a position where they face danger daily, creating concern for their safety and the safety of others.

Being injured on the job or having a mental issue due to the job can be stressful, as most do not know their next steps for moving forward. They had planned on staying in the career much longer than they were able to and now must face the unknown. When an officer knows they will never be released back onto full duty, they experience a sense of panic. They lose the security of a paying career they've enjoyed for so long. The loss of insurance further adds to their worries. They can no longer look forward to retirement.

At the same time, those they have worked with for so long may stop reaching out. Those they called friends and family for so long become distant. They quickly find out who their friends and family truly are during this kind of situation. They may try to hang on as long as possible; they may even try to hide their pain by taking painkillers so they can get back to work and not lose that security.

Unfortunately, for such officers, the addiction to painkillers begins here. They immediately return to light duty when they get off the pain meds. They push forward for fear of being medically retired and forgotten about. They do not want to be seen as useless, and they don't know what they'll do after leaving the department. In some cases, another officer will claim they are faking their injuries to get a payout or to receive their medical retirement. However, most officers who get injured do not want to retire. They are trying to get better, not be medically retired. Unfortunately, it becomes inevitable that their career is ending, and this fact is hard to swallow.

I have met officers from many different departments, and this situation seems to be the same everywhere. It can be stressful for the officer about to be forced into retirement. Not only do they have to worry about their future, but they also must put up with rumors and fight a battle against them. These rumors may even come from those they have been close with for several years—officers who know about their personal lives, have hung out with them after work and when off duty, and whose families they know. Yet, when the chips are down, it feels like these people all disappear, and the only time they talk to the injured officer is in passing in the hallway or when one of them needs something.

Another reason for narcotics addiction is to show other officers they are wrong, placing the injured officer back on the street where they feel they belong, working again with those who did the badmouthing. Unfortunately, being forced into retirement is a real eye-opener as to how close the brotherhood is or isn't. For the officers who talk shit, they don't realize or get the fact that retirement is way more stressful than anything else. We can put up with the schedule changes, losing time off, and the ever-changing policies, procedures, and laws. These challenges will have been ongoing from the first day on the job. Officers just learn to live with it all. We may not like it, but we learn to get a handle on it.

With the stress of being forced into retirement comes anxiety and depression—anxiety about working with those who do not believe your injury is real, the possibility of getting injured again, and what will happen if you are not placed in the position you had when you got hurt. Further anxiety kicks in about failing your family by not being able to go to work every day and make a living. Health insurance costs after retirement, college for your kids, and many other thoughts run through the mind of an officer in this position.

Not only are you dealing with all those concerns, but Human Resources also starts breathing down your neck to get you back on the road or out as quickly as possible. They don't want to be paying full salary for an officer sitting at a desk taking phone calls from pissed-off citizens. These calls are usually about trivial things like a neighbor getting paint on the wrong side of the fence or someone trying to kick a roommate out of their house because they ate food out of the refrigerator that wasn't theirs.

HR is about getting you fixed and back out as quickly as possible. Therefore, it may seem easier just to take the narcotics and hide the pain; that way, there is no worry or stress about your future, others aren't spreading rumors about you, and HR will stop hassling you about getting back on the road. Unfortunately, you can't do anything until the doctor assigned by the department releases you for duty, so there's that waiting process and all the appointments you must attend. Finally, the day comes when you receive the letter from Internal Affairs advising you are under investigation in reference to fitness for duty concerns.

Luckily, they are mostly there for you. They don't want to force you out any sooner than is needed. They want to make sure the proper steps are being taken to finalize the paperwork. Many came to me when this step came up, only because I had gone through it, and no higher-up gave any warning or prepared them for what was involved. Not knowing what you are walking into can be very stressful, especially if you have never had an official investigation against you.

In reality, this was the simplest step in my department. The IA sergeant advised me that the case would sit in a desk drawer and go nowhere as long as I was completing the proper procedures for my medical retirement. This is a scary part of the ordeal for those who have been to

IA before with negative results. Those previous results will have laid the groundwork for how IA works and may make the officer afraid they will be terminated before their official retirement. Many departments throughout the country don't have a plan for a medical retirement. This can send someone's head spinning, wondering how they will survive beyond their career; the retirement plan already in place isn't good enough to retire on. I couldn't imagine the fear in officers working under these conditions, having nothing beyond being forced out, no future pension, and very little in their retirement due to the rise and fall of the stock market.

When I was injured and facing the thought that I may not make it back out onto the road, I went through a short time of panic, as well. There was way too much to think about, and without the proper help or information, it scared the hell out of me. This was all due to the city doctor refusing to acknowledge the whole injury, focusing on one small part. That focus led to more physical therapy and further damage to other parts. All the while, I had to hear that the injury was not real. HR continuing to send letters advising I would be terminated if not back on the road within a year from the injury.

I was not the only one, though. Many other officers were going through the same harassment and disappointment of learning injuries were worse than the workman's compensation doctor thought. The possibility of never returning to the road was quite concerning. After seeing a specialist, I was told he would never release me to return to work; doing that would put others in danger. Therefore, in good conscience, he could not release me. This took a couple of weeks to sink in.

Like so many others, I went through all those fears mentioned earlier a second time. What was I going to do from here? Would my retirement be enough to support my family? How was I going to afford insurance for my family? What about college for my youngest child? After a couple of weeks, I realized I could do nothing about the situation, even after trying to figure out how to continue working with this injury. I knew there were other things I could get into. After all, I did plan just for this occasion. There was plenty of other work I could do, even if it meant going back into construction, which I did enjoy doing in the past.

The problem is that there are so many others in the same boat who don't come to that realization. Their stress and anxiety only increase. The only support you receive from your coworkers is a "good luck" and a "take care"—if you are lucky. The real support you get is from your family and maybe a couple of people from the department you are truly close to. It seems the only time a department is really there for an officer is if that officer has been shot in the line of duty. Otherwise, you become just another somebody who worked for the department once.

Taking everything into account, issues within one's personal and professional life, possible forced retirement, and even planning for life beyond retirement can all be causes for depression and anxiety far beyond the job itself. And these causes would be on top of the daily trauma, the constant changes in shifts and days off, and the ever-changing policies and procedures that must be followed. Everything just adds up to one big mess that may seem difficult to get out of.

Depression and Anxiety

The American Psychological Association (APA) defines depression as "extreme sadness or despair that lasts more than two weeks."[1] It's a condition that includes poor appetite, insomnia, low energy or fatigue, low self-esteem, poor concentration, and feelings of hopelessness. Anxiety is defined as the apprehensive anticipation of future danger or misfortune accompanied by a feeling of dysphoria or symptoms of tension. Anxiety can further be described as recurrent, unexpected panic attacks that cause constant concern.

Many officers have gone through both issues at some point in their careers—especially those with more than five years of experience. Newer officers may feel these same symptoms early in their career, as well, depending on their work area and how often they respond to critical incidents. What constitutes a critical incident for each officer is determined by the individual, not necessarily those in power such as commanders or other city officials. Everyone, even the civilian population, has their own definition of what is considered a critical incident—one that changes their lives in one way or another.

---

[1] American Psychological Association. (n.d.). *Depression*. American Psychological Association.
https://www.apa.org/topics/depression

Of course, official definitions can be followed when making decisions affecting others. However, first responders usually face more critical incidents than the general public. According to that article I mentioned earlier, an officer with a twenty-year career who has worked patrol for most of their career will face more than 800 critical incidents. First responders show up to calls nobody else wants to deal with. The general public would rather hear it on the news and think to themselves, "Man, I'm glad I don't have to deal with that. What a pity." Yet, much of the general public pays no attention to those responding to these incidents because those first responders "signed up to do the job." It's what we get paid to do, and therefore, we should be able to put our feelings aside and get on with our lives as if nothing has ever happened. This type of thinking is unfair to first responders.

As mentioned before, nobody ever thinks about the type of calls they will respond to when considering being a first responder. Much of what's on television makes the job look so glamorous, almost removing the possibilities of its horrific parts, like witnessing a suicide or homicide, showing up to a car accident so bad you can't identify the driver, or coming across a child who has been sexually assaulted. Well, officer-involved shootings really happen, fights really happen, murders really happen, and victims are really contacted as victims for the most part.

What television shows don't recreate are the aftereffects of such calls. These shows just portray everybody responding to the crime, standing around laughing and cutting up, holstering back up, and going on to the next call; this is not reality. All such calls have some impact, and when an officer is involved in a shooting, they don't just get to holster back up and respond to the next call. There are steps that have to be taken when an officer is involved in a shooting, and most departments force the officer to take a couple of weeks off afterward, for multiple reasons beyond the investigation. One main reason is so the officer can speak to a therapist and make sure that they will be okay after having taken the life of another. The stress of knowing that the incident will go in front of a grand jury at some point is very concerning, especially in today's world. There is the unknown of whether the shooting will be cleared as justified or whether future charges will be pending with jail time.

There is always the fear you will be charged with a felony crime and end up doing time in prison. The world has changed, and there are more officers being charged with homicide following officer-involved shootings; this is what society is calling for, and the courts are moving forward with those demands. The news doesn't talk much about what happens next. They talk about the version of the incident they receive from some bystander, not always the whole story at first—but hey, it's news.

I'm not saying they lie about anything, but they are quick to show only portions of incidents, or the one side told to them early on. They don't even wait until the investigation is completed. Even criminals get to have all sides told prior to conviction.

There have been a lot of stories in the news about departments with officers who are racist or use excessive force to create conditions so they can make an arrest. There have also been stories about officers posting stupid crap on Facebook, Instagram, and Twitter, and sending emails with objectionable materials within their department. There are some officers who are racist and will make comments or remarks about the people they have dealt with during their shift.

Now, I have to say one thing: every officer deals with their own version of racism for a brief period in their career.

That is true within any career, be it police work, firefighting, or construction. Everybody has some type of bias, whether against another's race, ethnicity, gender, or sexual preference. The difference is whether you act upon those biases or know how to control them. There is even bias shown against officers because of their race or gender. You must not allow the issue or bias to bother you in a way that can be seen by others.

Take control and realize those who caused those issues were not attacking you personally. It's the uniform that is not liked; police officers are a necessary evil, and that is well known even by those who support the career. We are taught to be the bigger person; it doesn't matter if someone is calling us names, swearing at us, or simply giving us the bird. We cannot act against that and lower ourselves to those levels. Officers posting on Facebook, Twitter, or whatever social media platform should know that they do not have the right to true freedom of speech. As most officers place their profession in their profile, they are still considered a representative of the organization they work for. Therefore, they do not have the right to post whatever they want and think it is okay. If you want to get fired quickly, that is definitely one way to do so.

At one time, it was easier for officers to get away with their actions because there was no use of cell phones, good security equipment—or security at all—to record their actions. No body cameras were worn while on duty. Those were more commonly found in traffic cars, mounted to dashboards and turned on only when a traffic stop was made. But nowadays, everyone has a cell phone, and there are surveillance cameras on nearly every corner. Body cameras are being issued by departments and reviewed almost daily to ensure officers are acting professionally and being courteous to everyone they come in contact with.

Gone are the days when someone complained about an officer and it could be swept under the rug because there was no evidence to prove any wrongdoings. The technology available in the world today allows us to record everything, and the evidence is there to prove someone guilty or innocent of what they are being accused of. However, there are still those who believe they can get away with their idiotic remarks or actions. These officers are the same ones with numerous complaints from previous negative interactions with the public, such as rude comments or use of force issues. There are many departments that have swept the issues under the rug and now must go back and take care of these previous complaints, especially when they should have been properly dealt with in the first place.

These are the officers giving the rest a bad name. First responders are held to a higher standard both on and off duty. It makes no difference whether there is a badge on your chest or not; you only treat people how you expect to be treated. If you expect to be treated like shit, I suppose such behavior is okay. However, there are some who think they are above the law simply because they are police officers. They justify their actions because they feel they have the right to do what they want.

Such police officers tend to be the bigger problem in such an honorable profession. Guess what, folks? This has never been the case, and it will continue not to be the case moving forward. You can't take illegal actions when off duty and expect to get off with just a slap on the wrist. You sure as hell can't treat people how you want because you wear a badge and think that block on your shoulder won't get knocked off at some point. The problem is when they do something illegal or stupid, they can't figure out how they got caught and try to act innocent.

They say stupid shit like, "But I was off duty, and nobody can tell me how to act off duty," or, "Nobody ever told me I couldn't." Common sense isn't as common as it used to be. Apparently, we have to hold the hands of the ignorant and stupid. It's no longer possible for an officer to drive home intoxicated and expect a ride home if they are pulled over. More officers are being charged for driving under the influence of alcohol because that is what society and supervisors expect to happen.

For those reading this, keep in mind that there is a small number of officers who behave this way and abuse their powers. We are talking less than one percent of the police population. Still, everyone wants to hold the whole group accountable. But it is up to the officers to police themselves. If you don't want to get in trouble or be linked to those idiots making the stupid decision, something must be said before it hits the news. The blue wall of silence is going away; more officers want to get rid of those who do not belong in the profession, and it is applauded.

Do not be afraid to speak up—you may be held just as accountable if nothing is said. Covering up for another holds the same punishment as committing the act, whether it's an internal violation or a violation of the law. All those officers are doing is making themselves look bad along with the rest of the police population, and I, for one, am tired of being blamed for the choices of a few.

There are still several old-timers either connected to their department after retirement or getting ready to retire that need to step up and start knocking some sense into these individuals. We, as an older generation, need to step up and take charge. Lessons need to be taught, whether from our own mistakes or someone else's. We need to educate those dishonoring the badge or get them the hell out and on to another career where every watchful eye in the nation isn't seeing what is happening.

Now, I understand officers are getting fed up with being treated like they are a necessary evil and an outcast because they wear a badge and uniform—but how does this change? It changes from within the organization and those exposed to the daily ridicule. It doesn't matter whether the officer is new and scared to say anything or has been in the department for a while and dealing with a long-time partner and friend.

If you think your job and career are worth losing for another person, if you're willing to lose your job just for being on the scene or around the conversation and not stopping the issue, then go for it. You don't deserve to wear your badge, anyway. But the actions making the news and giving a bad reputation must stop here and now. Your job is to go after criminals no matter who the hell it is. And no matter what color or race, we treat all with respect.

It all starts with our tone of voice: how we approach the situation and talk to those we contact. Instead of telling someone they are in the wrong area, how about asking if you could assist them with something? Maybe they are looking to commit a crime; but maybe they are lost and looking for their way around instead. You never know unless you talk to them. It can be figured out pretty damn quick. If you take the time to learn and read people, you will know the difference between someone who is actually lost and someone who is trying to talk themselves out of the contact so they can get on with their business.

There is not one single race committing crimes. If you are working with a racist officer, get away from them, as they will bring you down with them. Either you treat everybody as a criminal or treat everyone with respect until you make the determination of good or bad. There are many who go their whole career without getting in trouble for being rude, racist, or using excessive force.

These unproblematic officers may have received complaints for giving someone a verbal warning for a traffic violation or separating a couple during a domestic dispute because it made someone else mad, and an arrest wasn't made. It turns out all that was needed was some counseling. Remember, counseling and education are also part of the job we do. We provide marriage counseling and parenting tips, and we educate citizens on the laws. We do not make judgments or provide sentences; we are not Judge Dredd.

Okay, I will get off my soapbox now and continue with what I initially started. This is the reality of the job, and many, whether they agree or not, go through similar issues. Some officers will go their whole career and never see a homicide or deal with a victim of severe child abuse. Some will go through their whole career never drawing their weapon. But many will be dealing with all those incidents. Officers, for the most part, deal with the worst twenty minutes of people's lives whenever they are called. The same goes for many first responders in general. Firefighters don't just show up to a house to say hello. They are usually there because of a fire or a medical emergency during which someone has lost everything, or they show up to help when a family member has found their loved one dead.

Police officers respond to those same types of calls and then some. They respond to domestic violence disputes where the victim had been severely beaten and/or raped, sexual assault calls for both adults and juveniles, child abuse cases, car accidents involving death, officer-down situations, and so much more. After a time, this begins to wear on a person, and they go through bouts of depression and anxiety. But not all will be willing talk to someone about what is bothering them.

They just put it in the back of their head and move on to the next call. What normally happens is they end up thinking about those calls when they get home later that night and have the time. It is very hard not to take your work home with you. It's not like getting yelled at by your boss for not getting a presentation ready on time for the next sales meeting. Officers think about the dead child in a car accident, or being victims of abusive parents—every injured child who is the same age as one of their own.

This hits very close to home and causes anxiety and stress. They may not want to leave their house because of the dangers that could happen to their own family. They become depressed because of images constantly running through their mind of what they encountered during their shift or the constant nightmares they have every time they try to go to sleep.

They get to a point in their life where they don't want to do anything on their time off because they just don't want to deal with people anymore. Therefore, they end up staying home and losing interest in the things they like to do or hobbies they once enjoyed. When their spouses want to go out and do something, they have no interest, causing distance and separation from their own family. Sometimes, this is the cause of divorce; there is no interest in doing things together as a couple or with the family. This seclusion makes officers feel alone.

There are officers who make sure to do things they enjoy on their days off. Still, the fact remains that many lose that interest if they don't receive help on time. They may break promises to their children or other family members, cancel plans at the last minute, or just refuse to make plans. Part of this is because they never know if court will arise, if last-minute department training will be required, or if extra coverage on a shift will be necessary.

They have no desire to do anything but relax, watch television, and think of anything but work. Besides these limited activities, they worry about their week or issues within the department. Some suffer anxiety attacks over the mere thought of having to go to work, afraid of what may be next. They may start calling in sick more often or pretend to be sick to go home early. They may try to hide during their shift, placing themselves on a bullshit call so they appear busy and dispatch won't bother them. They may prefer to stay home and isolated in the safety of their own house. It can be hard to get out of this pattern if not caught early enough or dealt with at all.

These are things to think about while deciding whether to become a first responder. It goes beyond what we watch on television. These issues go beyond personal live and will extend into professional life, as well. When officers are constantly put under stressful situations, they tend to act out, needing to take their frustrations out somewhere. They take their frustrations out on the public and the suspects they deal with, become verbally abusive to victims and witnesses, and overreact to situations where they may deem something to be dangerous when it actually is not.

They may arrest individuals using more force than necessary just because it's a way to relieve stress and frustration or because they are tired of dealing with the same calls every day. The public may take a hit because it may be members of the public causing stress and frustration. Look at how some officers have treated the public, which has gained more visibility through social media. However, officers using excessive force have been happening since long before now.

Again, in the past, we didn't have social media to post our videos or the option of pulling out a mini camera or smartphone, recording, and then sending it directly to news sources. There are members of the public who have consistently been abusive to law enforcement, even before cell phones were a thing and long before phones had cameras. Officers feel the need to fight back, either verbally or physically, when they are feeling threatened or frustrated. When stress and anxiety rear their ugly heads, it can multiply the frustration even further, and when the public acts in a threatening or disrespectful manner, it can intensify, causing overreaction and physical violence. The community does not think about things like that.

The community thinks law enforcement is a necessary evil that's only there to protect them when they need to be protected. So, when an officer does their job as per their job description, the person being contacted, whether through a traffic stop or as a suspect of a crime, can become verbally abusive. They will talk about how the police work for them and they pay the officer's salary. They will follow this by telling the officer that they need to go find something else to do. "Go find a real criminal instead of harassing an innocent person." Imagine dealing with that on a daily basis—not from everybody, but many times throughout the day, every day you work. It has a tendency to wear on officers and make them defensive to the point of total and complete frustration.

Besides dealing with the public in a negative manner, there are changes within their department by means of policies and procedures, changes in command, changes of uniforms, turnover in manpower, or complaints coming in. Even more of an issue today than ever before is the lack of manpower. There are not enough officers on the street, either due to a lack of interest or fear of wearing the uniform. Therefore, those still working the job have to cover the holes and the extra shifts. There is also the stress of dealing with officers who make bad decisions, who just don't have any business wearing the badge or the uniform, or who don't care about officer safety.

This can be stressful to many officers who take their job to heart, live their lives the same on and off duty in a respectful manner, and make sure every action they complete on calls is as expected by not only the department but also the community. For some officers who are field-training officers (FTO), there is the stress of training new officers who have no prior experience. The FTO knows all blame falls back on them when the recruit messes up a call, whether through their paperwork or actions.

The FTO knows they will take the heat if the recruit screws up bad enough to where disciplinary action is required, too. They are also the officers trying to make sure the recruit does not quit while in training. Manpower within a department is a requirement so that existing officers within the department do not get worn down. At one of the departments where I worked, when we would lose one or two officers, we worked a minimum of sixty hours of overtime every pay period until those positions were filled.

Sometimes, it would take months to fill those positions, wearing down all of us. Burnout would become an issue because we would get called in to cover shifts and lose scheduled time off. On top of that, court always seemed to happen on days off. It was tough, but we managed to make it happen. There are several departments where this continues to be an issue, with forced overtime and loss of vacation time due to the lack of manpower.

Burnout is a major issue for smaller agencies, as well, because there is no way for an officer to move around within the department to get away from the everyday grind. Not every department has the opportunity for officers to be promoted within their department; those who are promoted have been at the department for a long time and have earned that right in their position. There is also the issue of newer officers working the same shift for several years because those senior officers would rather work a day shift or swing shift, leaving newer officers stuck in the midnight shift.

Officers working for larger departments have a better opportunity to move into a different unit or change shifts. These departments provide opportunities to try something new, such as a gang unit, narcotics unit, investigations, or even promotion through a testing process where seniority has no advantage. Now I'm talking about city departments; sheriff's departments have added stress every election year.

There is still a concern that a new sheriff will be elected and come in to clean house, meaning deputies can be fired on the spot without cause.

This is not a common practice or occurrence, but it could still happen, and there is no telling whether it will or not. Similar to city departments, some sheriff departments provide deputies the opportunity to move around and promote within the department through testing, and some do not because they are too small for movement to be an option.

Burnout is not only caused by being unable to move around in a department or having to work excess overtime. It can also be caused by the constant stress of the day-to-day job, the calls for service, the changes within the department, and the worry of whether you will receive a complaint. Besides these on-the-job worries, officers also deal with the looming threat of someone trying to kill them. As an officer, you are expected to take all these worries home with you every night.

We are taught from Day One that we have to live our lives like we are doing the job at all times. We are first responders 24/7. We never let our guard down. We are always looking over our shoulder. We are always willing to run into an incident, whether we are on duty or not. That is who we are. The problem is we don't know how to shut that off from one day to the next, even when on vacation. We get used to carrying our equipment everywhere we go, whether it is a gun, first aid supplies, or rescue equipment.

When we do the same thing every day and are always watching for that danger, it can wear us down. We begin to try and figure out what else we can do. We don't want to go to work. We want to find something outside of being a first responder. This may last a short and brief moment or could go longer. Changing things up in your job is very helpful in dealing with burnout issues. Finding different hobbies or interests on your days off that encourage you to concentrate on something other than the job could be of help, as well.

Burnout can also be caused by hypervigilance. This is the constant awareness of being always on watch for danger, whether you are working at home or out in public. There are some officers who have learned that danger is not lurking around every corner, so they are able to relax while at home, in public, or on vacation. These are the same officers who will still notice when something is not right— that sixth sense, if you will. Still, these more seasoned officers don't live every day like they are always in danger.

A large portion of officers are always on watch. They won't sit with their back to the door. They want to make sure they can see everyone within a room. They don't feel comfortable in large crowds around people they don't know. It is too hard to keep an eye on everyone in a large crowd. There are some who won't go to a movie theater or allow their children to go to school where there is open access and no one inside the school whose job is to identify people before allowing entry. Some won't go to malls because the space is too wide-open and there are too many corners for potential criminals to hide in. Anxious officers have their reasons. Perhaps they ended up on a call where the situation was bad enough to make them nervous everywhere they go.

Types of Stressful Calls for Service

Imagine having to respond to a domestic violence call where the victim has been assaulted so badly they can't open their eyes or even move their mouth because their face is too swollen. When you respond to the scene, you recognize the victim and the offender from responding in the past; yet the victim returned to the suspect after release from the arrest during the prior response. The last time was just as bad; the bruises from it are still visible. Yet here you are again—and this time, a small child is involved. The fight started over the suspect severely abusing the young child, who is upstairs in a bedroom, bruised and bleeding. During the assault on the child, the victim stepped in to take the strikes for the child. You end up arresting the suspect again, knowing damn well the victim will take the suspect back after release from jail. You can do nothing about it except give the victim some information and pamphlets on how to make sure the victim and child can be protected in the future. The problem is, you or another officer will be back, and you just hope it's not in the form of a homicide.

Most police officers find it uncomfortable to listen to detailed descriptions from the victim about the abuse. It's not something that can be taken easily. The situation becomes even more difficult when the victim is a juvenile male or female. It is bad enough that the suspect may be a relative of some type, like a stepparent, uncle, biological parent, or cousin,. The officer may need to read an explicit journal, like the one kept for seven years by the young girl who was repeatedly abused by her stepdad, involving the very detailed acts performed on them or the acts they had to perform on the offender.

On top of that, the biological parent may choose not to believe the child because the offender is the one who brings in the money and provides the roof over their head; therefore, the victim is called a whore, slut, or liar. Yet, knowing they will not be believed by the parent and possibly have to testify in court, they report it anyway because perhaps they have a younger sibling they feel needs protecting. They are afraid the sibling has been molested or assaulted, as well, and this is the only way to protect that younger sibling.

Now, if you have a child around the same age or younger, you start to worry about them being around other family members alone because something like this could happen to them. You start to think how you would react in this type of situation and become angry, and you take this home with you at the end of your shift, all the anger and concern.

Every officer must perform traffic stops during their day. They may not even necessarily be looking for stops to make but see someone make the mistake of running a red light, speeding, driving aggressively, or driving while intoxicated. You have many eyes watching to see if you will stop this crazy driver, and you know if you don't, someone will call in and say you are not doing your job. So, you make the traffic stop, not knowing what you are getting into or who you will be making contact with. This uncertainty has nothing to do with race.

The driver decides how the traffic stop is going to happen. They could either be respectful and take what ticket they receive because they will have their day in court, and they understand that and know they were in the wrong. Or you may be dealing with someone who gets offensive immediately and begins trying to belittle you. You may be pulling over a violent offender who is ready to do whatever is necessary to keep this traffic stop from continuing and possibly going to jail. Traffic stops are the most stressful calls because officers deal with the unknown. Until you make contact with that driver and any potential passengers, you have no information on them and no understanding of their intent.

Those intending to hurt you can be of any race, age, or gender; you just never know. However, your views will change the first time someone shoots at you from inside their car or intends to shoot at you from the car. Their reasons may not even be known. It could be due to the driver having been arrested for something, and now they are taking their aggression out on any officer working for the department. For the most part, drivers do not intend to hurt anyone, but they get angry or upset for being pulled over and take that out on officers.

That is just a taste of calls an officer can receive during their shift or work week. Most of the public has no idea of what really happens—except, again, what they see on television shows. Even the television show *Cops* does not air until it has been edited, and only certain things are aired to make it look more interesting. Officers get called many different names besides "Officer" or their real name. They are verbally abused many times during their career, and if people don't think that it wears on them, they are mistaken.

The average person in public would become very upset if they were called what I have heard officers being called, names bad enough to start a physical altercation between two people. Yet police officers must keep their cool. They are not allowed to let people in the community see them mad, upset, or stressed. We must go around being all stoic, as if nothing ever gets to us—but it does. Officers are human, too. We take it all home and then return the next day and start all over again.

Interdepartmental Stress

Departments review policies and procedures almost every year. A department may decide that all complaints will go to the Internal Affairs division to be reviewed, no matter how petty or small those complaints may be. The procedure used to be such that a lieutenant or sergeant could handle smaller complaints. However, that didn't seem to work for the agenda of those in charge, so it changed. This could include someone calling to complain because they received a verbal warning for a traffic stop and feel the officer was just wasting their time by pulling them over.

There may be changes in the use of force policy, such as dictating when use of force can and can't be used. Policy dictates when a police officer is allowed to use a Taser or pepper spray or when they are allowed to go hands-on with a suspect. There may be changes in policy on whether you can chase a vehicle that runs from a traffic stop or not. There may be changes in the uniform so that officers from one department look different from others. There might be specific directions for speaking to suspects, victims, or witnesses. There might be demands regarding how many citizen contacts must be made during a shift or how many traffic stops are required in a week or month.

Most everyone below the chief's office really has no idea these changes are being considered; they are brought up during a briefing and take effect immediately. Changes may be made within ranks; someone who didn't deserve that promotion may be promoted, and now you must work under them. Someone gets promoted while you are being passed up for it, even though they don't fully understand the job. Many changes are made within a department, and even more with a change in command.

New chiefs always want to make their mark, separate themselves from the rest, and let everyone know who is in charge. Officers don't like change, especially within their own department. They also don't like being forced to perform in a specific way with expectations that can lower their chance for promotions and/or raises or that may put them in danger. They are expected to get over that, though, as well. They aren't allowed to voice their opinions or concerns once the decision has been made. If they are heard doing so, they risk being reprimanded in one way or another.

As I've mentioned, court dates always seem to come up on days off. It doesn't matter if you have plans or not. Officers must show up for court no matter what they have planned or with whom they've made plans. Sometimes, these subpoenas are given within just a few days before the hearing, allowing little time to prepare. You know you need to review the case before the hearing, so you take your work home with you and do it during your off time.

You cancel plans for the day so you can go to court; however, when you get to the courthouse, you are told the case had been postponed or canceled. Now, your day off has been taken away, and the family is upset because of this case, so you try to make the best of things. If you are working the graveyard shift and this case was between shifts, you now have to get back home and try to get some sleep before the next shift starts, which can leave you tired and agitated.

You may take that agitation home and take it out on those around you, causing even more problems. If you forget about a court date or don't wake up in time, you are not only violating policy, but you are also violating a court order. So, there is no choice. The attorneys who subpoenaed you have no concern about what you had planned or the sleep you need. They will schedule cases on their own time. If you are

351

lucky, you will find out the case has been postponed or canceled before you show up for it.

Of course, there is also the never-ending change in the shift you have to work. Work shifts can change yearly, or they may change more often depending on the agency. It does not always depend on the shift you want to work; it depends on seniority and what is left. Officers with higher seniority are the ones who get the shifts they want, and it could take years to get to that level and get your favorite work shift.

This type of work routine can be hard on the family, as well. In most cases, the officer's spouse will try to keep their kids quiet while the officer sleeps during the day. If you work weekends, you have to plan things to do in the middle of the week. If your spouse works, you may not have the same time off. Working a swing shift may mean you hardly see your kids if they are in school. You may see them for a few minutes in the morning but will likely be off to work before they get home, and they'll be in bed and sleeping when you get home. Working odd shifts is stressful not only for you, but also for your family who would like to see more of you.

One of the departments I worked for made it mandatory for every officer to attend a seminar where the speaker kept talking about letting things go. It's just that simple. Don't get over-invested in the changes made in the department, how you are treated on the street, or the last-minute court date you are required to attend. Don't get over-invested in the small things in life, personal or professional. Just let things go. Leave it all behind. He talked about changes made in departments, saying these changes are necessary and officers must live with leadership decisions. You have to expect there are going to be changes.

The officers don't make the rules; they are expected to live with them. If those rules are beyond what the officer can live with, they should change departments or retire from the force altogether. *Let it go!*

Well, I'm here to tell you that that is not a simple task. Officers who have been with the same department for ten, fifteen, or twenty years are already invested in the department and changes made. Having this amount of time spent within a department, officers like and are used to how things are, which is one reason they stay for so long. It's not because there were constant changes; it's because there was stability and things remained the same.

Once upon a time, a department I worked for did not have department patches on their shirts. Its chief decided patches were necessary because he could not identify the difference between his officers and the adjoining city's officers. This did not sit well with the older officers; they knew who they worked for, and it wasn't their fault the chief couldn't tell the difference. They enjoyed not having those patches for many reasons. Besides that, the officers now had to pay out of their own pockets to have all these shoulder patches put on their shirts—and if not done by a certain time, they could and would be reprimanded.

So, for someone to tell officers to just let things go is ridiculous. This is someone who never invested in any one department themselves and thought it should be the same for those who invested many years into the department and their career. Not everyone has an exit strategy. Therefore, they want what they want, and the changes make it difficult to enjoy the job they have as they once did.

This patches change was the first of many coming to the department, even after I started. The department made many cuts at the patrol level, including loss of holiday time and shift differential and changes in policy regarding the use of the Taser. New policies related to tattoos were also implemented. These policies stated during which times of the year officers were allowed to wear short-sleeved shirts and when officers needed to wear long-sleeved shirts, along with many other changes.

I wasn't with this department for very long, but I can see how those officers who had been would've felt like they were losing a lot. They enjoyed working graveyard or swing shifts because, for one, they were used to the shift and could receive differential pay—a little extra for working those shifts. All the holidays they were getting now paid less, so the time they would save up to take off later in the year was cut, shortchanging their plans altogether. But according to the speaker we had to listen to, they all had to deal with it and not get over-invested in the changes. This would be the new norm, and they may as well get over the fact that the changes would take place.

My second department also made changes during my time there. Those of us who had been there for a while didn't enjoy them much. It wasn't easy to just get over it. Whether a supervisor agrees with the changes or not, they must sell the ideas to the rest of the officers and show their support for the department's decisions. They don't have the option to voice their opinions or share their concerns, either; this makes being in a supervisor position more difficult. They are in a position where they must remain on the side of the department, creating more distance between their officers and themselves.

Most officers who join a department plan on staying there until they retire. The moment they sign on, they are already invested in the decisions and changes forced upon them. So, when negative changes are made, like loss of pay, loss of time off, and so on, they will get upset because the stability in their lives and careers gets disturbed. There is no stability in calls for service because you never know what will happen from one call to the next—which can be exciting. It's not exciting, however, when workings within the department are constantly changing and being shaken up. People are going to be upset, and there's no way around that. To tell officers not to get over-invested in the decisions of the department is like telling a child not to cry when you take that sucker out of their mouth and throw it away.

I am not placing actual statistics into these issues; they are out there and can be found easily. These issues are being described through my own life experiences and those of the many other officers I've met and known throughout the police field. Many articles can be found on these same topics, written and studied by those within law enforcement. You may say things like, "This isn't me; I have control of everything," or "This will never happen to me. I am more careful than that, with a supportive department and family." One never knows when these areas will become issues.

The issues may appear without you noticing them developing within you. They creep in so slowly that there won't be any immediately notable changes. But I will tell you something: your family, friends, coworkers, and supervisors will notice. These people are around you enough to know when you are just not right but may be too afraid to say anything. When something was said in the past, maybe you got upset with them, yelled at them, told them they were the ones changing. In the case of coworkers, maybe you just tried to get them to quit being a cop, retire, and find something else.

So many officers don't recognize the issues. No, you have not always been this way. The job changes a person, just like being a firefighter or paramedic changes those people. Throughout their careers, they observe trauma, chaos, hate, changes, and lives that have been taken. All first responders learn to adapt to those changes; we make ourselves less vulnerable to emotions.

We can't let others see us upset because we are the strong ones. We run in while everyone else runs out. We won't even make the time to let those emotions out; somebody may walk in while this is happening, and we can't allow that, either. So, we bottle it all up inside until one day, we explode with anger at the wrong time, either to the citizens we deal with daily or to our family members— usually a spouse.

We need to pay attention to the emotional signs of exhaustion and burnout. Some of those signs include depression, anxiety about going to work, cynicism or pessimism, apathy, detachment, becoming easily angered, feeling hopelessness or dread, lack of motivation, decline in productivity (both personal and professional), and difficulty concentrating. This list is not something we should only be watching for within ourselves, but also in others we work with.

Our loved ones and close friends may identify these signs of exhaustion before we can. They might need to bring these problems to the forefront and inform us about them. When someone points out those issues to you, anger about it is not what the reaction should be. The reaction must be to take a step back, look at yourself in the mirror, and identify what is being told to you. Acknowledge that you are no longer the person you were before getting into this career— or into any career where you may face the same dangers and stressors.

The mindset that causes people not to seek professional counseling is changing. This change has taken a long time to get through to officers, especially the older officers who have been doing the job for a long time. It was believed for many years that talking to a therapist was a weakness. It meant you couldn't handle your emotions and that something was wrong with you. It was also feared that the information you would give to a therapist might get back to your department, which could force you off the street and onto a desk job or, worse, retirement.

There was a time when your coworkers may have thought you were weak and couldn't handle the job anymore. It isn't that way now. Nothing could be said or done to convince hesitant officers to ask for help. Most thought, "How could someone who has never been in the types of situations I have been in possibly be able to help me? How could they understand when their work involves staying in an office all day and learning about the world from the news they watch at night?" Unfortunately, there are still many who hold onto this same thinking. They refuse to talk to anyone, letting a lifetime of pain, stress, and anxiety eat at them until they can't take anymore, ending up going off the deep end and getting fired—or worse, taking their own lives to get rid of it all.

Over the course of my career, I have lost a total of seven friends to suicide. Most of them never said anything about what was bothering them. They let everyone around them believe everything was okay. They put on that strong face, allowing nobody—and I mean *nobody,* including family—to see their pain. It was a complete surprise to everybody when we were notified they had taken their own lives. Of course, we all blamed ourselves for not paying close enough attention to any signs that may have been visible.

Remember, officers who take their own lives don't go through the normal psychological profile of telling at least one person of their intent, giving away personal possessions, or leaving notes. They all understand the consequences if anything like this is noticed and mentioned to a supervisor. They know they could be stopped; the department may take away their weapons until counseling is sought out and yields a successful and positive outcome.

This, too, would mean they would be taken off the road. They would either be placed into light duty or forced to take time off until they were deemed safe to return to normal work.

Saying nothing ensures they have the ability to be successful at their attempt, and nobody will have to worry about them ever again. As I mentioned earlier, they don't think about the outcome for those around them, such as friends and family. They only think about taking care of the pain and not being a burden to either themselves or others.

Again, thankfully, counseling is becoming less of a horrible thought. Officers are getting a better understanding that it is there to help and not hinder. The suicide rate is still high, meaning there are not enough officers taking advantage of the opportunities available to help them. For those still thinking that counseling is a terrible thing, think again. Take the help provided—especially when it could help you and your family.

Counselors are not allowed to share with the department you work for anything you talk about— especially counselors not related to or working closely with your department. If you don't feel comfortable talking to a therapist, talk to someone close to you, whether a friend or family member. Sometimes, getting the information out and getting advice from someone close can make all the difference. You never know what information someone can provide. There is always help available if you look hard enough for it. Realize it isn't just you, and that there are so many others in the same position who are willing to help however they can.

I once believed that talking to a counselor would provide no real results. Instead, after five years of never dealing with the death of a friend, I found the one person who would listen and be able to help me get out of the dark place I was in for so long. My wife has stayed strong by my side. She knows it is a daily struggle, even to this day, but she has stood by me through my worst.

Finding Your Way Out of Your Own Head

Many first responders have interests or hobbies where they can find themselves and escape from the stress at the end of their workweek or workday. Sometimes, that interest is lost after time because the stress, anxiety, or depression is so strong they find no joy in what was once enjoyed. But we all need a way to escape our problems and stresses other than alcohol, narcotics, or even the television. Television can also cause psychological harm. Watching the news all the time can be depressing; all it does is cover the negative stuff in the world.

As police officers, or first responders in general, we already see enough of the negative and trauma throughout our work week. Trying to keep up with all the issues in the world just adds negativity to one's mind, which is unnecessary. It seems that there are very few positive news stories about officers. They seem to focus on the negative and will cover that information before they even have all the facts of the case—and face it: this does not help society respect the position. It feeds on the negative, making us all look bad.

It's all about the ratings and nothing about respecting those involved. They don't think about how an officer is affected when they get involved in a shooting or when someone loses their life due to actions of the officer that weren't intended to go the way they did. Our local, state, and federal officials are providing no help in this matter either; they want to appease those who are screaming the loudest without helping others understand an action is still under investigation and details of an open case cannot be talked about, just like details would not be given about any other suspect until files have been charged. That would make for an unfair trial if it were to go too far. All in all, *turn off the damn television* and find something else to ease your mind and tensions!

Find something else to do. Force yourself to find new interests or hobbies if your old ones don't work anymore. Doing this may cause you to develop hobby ADD.... I'm joking, of course! This is where you start hobbies or pursue interests to find out which ones you like and don't like. However, you don't want to eliminate the older hobbies altogether because you may rediscover your interest in those later. Use these activities to make time for yourself or give time to your family while doing something you enjoy.

Get outdoors and go hiking, camping, fishing, or hunting if you don't want to be close to many people. These interests can help you get into areas with few people around. If others are around, there are ways to maintain distance from them. If you once liked to exercise but think gyms are too crowded, then take up hiking, riding bikes, or running. Put workout equipment in your backyard and exercise there; that way, you can get physical activity and fresh air during warm weather. You can even join a sports team with a few good friends and play softball, volleyball, bowling, or golf.

If you don't want to leave your house, you can build models of old cars, ships, planes, or whatever your favorite thing may be. Hell, tanks are also fun to build. Learn to tie flies for fishing or make artificial lures. Write a book. Rebuild an old car you may once have wanted. These are just some activity ideas to give you things to look forward to.

A friend of mine is a beekeeper. I enjoy reading his posts and seeing his excitement on his Facebook page. However, he also likes to ski in the wintertime and admits it is a time for him not to think about the stress or the calls he had to deal with over the week. There are so many things one could do to escape from the everyday stressors of the job. You must find that one thing to help you escape, such as learning to play an instrument or learning a new language, or even going back to school and learning something completely away from criminal justice or the field you are currently in—cooking, education, or archaeology, for example.

If talking to others or a professional does not appeal to you, or if the idea makes you uncomfortable, start a journal. Each day, put your thoughts onto paper—not just your wild imagination, but what happened throughout your day, what was good about it and what was bad. Write down how certain calls made you feel, whether good or bad, what changes took place in the department, and how those changes will affect you now and in the future.

Each time I returned to school to get that next degree, it helped give me something else to focus on, as I know it did for so many others; this was just another escape for me, not having to think about work or personal issues I may have been dealing with. Now, don't get me wrong. I am not saying these are the exact ways to relieve stress or anxiety. What I am saying is you need to find an alternative to alcohol, drugs, and the television. It is good to get things out, whether to a therapist, friends, family members, or a journal. You can't just hold it all in and hope it disappears over time. It won't.

Since finishing school, I have found other ways of dealing with the trauma I endured, writing this book to help others has been therapeutic getting it out for other to read. Teaching college classes in criminal justice also helps with thinking I may be helping future officers understand how to cope with the trauma they will be facing. Fishing is a skill that takes focus and an understanding of the beauty that surrounds me.

Please note that I am not a licensed therapist. I have had training through my education and working closely with other therapists who are licensed. I have also offered advice and suggestions to those who have felt comfortable opening up to me, asking me for ideas to escape their reality. They want to know what they need to do to get away from their everyday world, where their stress is overwhelming, and they are in a depressed state of mind.

There will be many who call my ideas bullshit, and that is fine. There will be licensed therapists who will say that my ideas or suggestions are not proper, which is also fine. For those officers who say it is bullshit: If you have never been affected by calls you have been involved in, then you probably haven't been to a crime scene where the victim reminds you of someone close to you, or a scene that was so horrific it made you step back and wonder if this job was right for you.

However, then again, maybe there is a little psychosis going on there, and you enjoy those calls or scenes a little too much. This will be the same for firefighters, paramedics, emergency room doctors, nurses, and any other first responder falling into this category. Either that, or you are just cold-blooded and nothing affects you. As for any professional therapist, it is easy to read a book and tell someone how they should think or act, tell someone something is not their fault, or take money from the insurance company or the customer as long as they continue to attend their sessions.

Some of the first responders who have taken their own lives had been to therapy many times, and the outcome was still the same. They just figured out how to lie enough to make the therapist feel comfortable saying they were doing better. In the same respect, there is no shame in talking to a professional or someone who is not. Let others know the issues; do not just make people wonder, guess, and worry.

I see ads and posts telling us to say something to someone when we do not want to go on. They come from people who have never been in that mindset, not understanding how difficult saying something may be. I will repeat what I said earlier: in my twenty years of law enforcement, seven officers whom I considered friends killed themselves. Nobody around them had any idea of their intentions.

Two of them were seeing a therapist and on medication for depression. The therapists did not know they were intending to take their own lives either; this came from the therapists' mouths. I am telling you: there is no shame in admitting the one thing you don't want to admit if you are at that point. What is it you tell people thinking about attempting suicide? There are more people in your life than just yourself to think about. No, it is not better to end it all to help them or keep them from thinking you are worthless or a hindrance. There are so many others who will feel the pain of you killing yourself to ease your burdens: your spouse, children, other family members, coworkers, and friends. I know you have repeatedly been told to speak up, and you must. There is no way you can be helped without saying something. Even if you think you are too far gone, it is never too late to fix your problems or the demons in your own head.

Here's the dilemma: many get into a phase within their own thoughts where they just think about how they act or what they have come to believe is normal. They have been in this dark place for so long that they don't think there is any help for them—or they think there is nothing they need help for. They wear a mask so regularly that nobody else can see they have troubles. When someone goes on so long, they grow dark within themselves to such an extent that nobody and nothing else matters. Just themselves. Still, they don't recognize the issue. They don't accept any help. They refuse to change who they are.

Listen to others around you. Hear what they say so the proper measures can be taken. Being stubborn is not going to help you or anybody close to you. It just worsens everything and will continue to get worse, no matter your thoughts. If it were possible for everyone to take care of their issues and deal with the stresses by themselves, then tell me why there are so many suicides among first responders—not just law enforcement, but all of them. Look around and ask for the help that is needed. There are many resources available. All you have to do is reach for it.

For Family Members and Friends of First Responders

This section is for the family or friends of first responders who may have noticed changes in their loved ones but do not quite understand why or how to handle them. There is a reason you don't hear about everything that goes on while your officer is on duty. Believe it or not, they think they are protecting you from the worry and the reality of the world that surrounds you and them. Whether you knew your significant other or friend prior to them getting into the field or got to know them after they had started, I am sure there have been days where you have worried about that person—or at least wondered what was going on with them.

I am sure there have been days when they've come home and not felt like talking or being involved in any conversation in general. They may come home and be in a bad mood or easily agitated, or they may come home without saying a word and grab their child or significant other and just hug them with a look of worry or sorrow in their eyes. Yet, you have no idea what the problem is or why they have come home this way. They do not talk about their day; nor do they want to. They may simply want to come home to silence. They may not even want to watch television because the news might come on and remind them of something that happened during their shift. Worse yet, you may see something they had been involved in that would make you worry.

These are the days they are trying to forget, put in the back of their mind in a dark little box, and lock away. But you know something is wrong, and you don't know how to fix the issue. This can be scary for you, as well. It may also irritate you that they never talk about their day or their week. But you know they love you—though they may have a hard time saying even that. It has nothing to do with you or what you did or did not do. It all has to do with what happened during their shift, whether it's a call for service, a department change, a complaint they received, or a hundred other things they don't think you need to know about. They'll keep it all inside. Again, this is their way of protecting you from whatever they think you need to be protected from. There have been plenty of times when I would not talk about what happened on my shift or during the week. I knew others who did the same thing, upsetting their spouse who'd wanted to hear about what happened and not miss out on something interesting.

However, when your loved one has a good day, you'll know that, as well. They will come home and happily talk about what happened during the day. They will recall how they had to talk to some kids because their parents wouldn't discipline them and called the cops to do it for them. They expect the cops to raise their children and have that stern talk in hopes the child won't act up again. Your loved one may even talk about a complaint their supervisor received because someone was let off with a verbal warning for a traffic violation, and the driver was irritated because now their time was wasted.

Fortunately, most officers have several good days. Hopefully, this happens more than the bad days—but that's not always the case. Most of the time, they are just dealing with the day-to-day stupidity of people, and it makes them laugh. They may even laugh and joke about something you may find a little disturbing to be laughing about; however, that is how they get through their day sometimes.

Humor is the key to being able to do the job for so long. There is so much they see that the public does not know about or does not want to know about. They sometimes get through it by making fun of the situation or the call. There may be good things that happen that they have not heard about in the news or on social media and that they are proud of. They may want to share those good things with you, or the things that made them feel good about the job on a given day.

The calls during their shift that they don't want to talk about are those where there's no humor to help them cope. These may be the calls they never want to talk about. They just want to put them in the back of their mind, hoping not to have to think about them again—unless they have to revisit them in court or have to explain to their family or friends something related that was seen in the news. Don't push them to talk about it. There are some things that talking won't help with healing or processing what happened. They are keeping quiet for a reason. The call may have been heinous, and telling you about it, what the officer saw or had to do, will only cause you to get upset.

When your loved one has a bad day, the best thing you can do is allow them their space. No words are even needed. Be in the same room, but don't push them to talk about whatever is bothering them. Talk about the good things in your day if they are willing to listen, and allow them to process their troubles before they talk to you. If they don't respond to you, getting upset will only make things worse. Trust me: they are listening to you and hearing what you are talking about. They just don't feel like talking back.

Remember, they see and deal with things you only watch on television and in movies. Your fears are their reality. They have talked to many people throughout the day and sometimes just don't feel like talking anymore; but they are listening. Don't offer any suggestions of what they should do or how they should feel. Telling somebody everything will be okay is like telling a newborn baby to get up and walk. It just won't happen. But eventually, the child will learn to take that first step, just like that officer or first responder will put the problem in the back of their mind and continue on with their life. One thing to remember is that their day consists of dealing with the worst of things and having to respond to the next call without having the ability to process what just happened on the current one. Their home time is the time they get to process and get away from the world, and you must let them.

In the same respect, in time, it will take your help to make sure they don't lose interest in the things they like to do. Keep them interested, and allow them to find hobbies or interests they can do with the family, their friends, or even alone. There is nothing wrong with doing things together, but sometimes it's just good to allow someone the time to get away and enjoy life again. Let them know you will be there next to their side no matter what.

Many spouses don't understand why officers don't talk about their problems or why they get upset so easily. This lack of understanding can cause many more problems within the household, along with more anxiety and depression in the officer. It can affect the mental health of other members of the family, beyond spouses and children. When your loved one says they are protecting you, it means they don't want you to worry about their safety. They don't want to scare you or keep you from worrying more than you already do.

We all know how our family and friends worry for our safety, whether we make it home in one piece or not. But we don't want your fears to get any worse than they already are. The stress on the family is just as difficult as the stress on the officer. Family members and friends are always concerned about what could happen during a shift—that officers may not make it home or that they may get a phone call saying their loved one is in the hospital. Trust me when I say that is the last thing the officer wants, as well. That is something they never expect or intend to have happen. The goal is always to make it home at the end of each shift. Officers understand the possibility of them not making it home is always there, and that makes them worry, too.

To keep this worry from getting worse, they may distance themselves from friends and family. This is just a defense mechanism that seems to make going to work easier. It helps them concentrate on the job and what is going on around them instead of worrying about what will happen to their friends and family if something goes wrong. That fear is still there, and that distance remains because, in time, it becomes normal and easy. As mentioned earlier, pushing the officer to act or talk can cause arguments and drive them further away. In their mind, now they have a reason to distance themselves even more. And now that they are angry, it makes it even easier to go to work. The best thing that can be done is to let the officers sort it out themselves. Get them to spend time with you, let them have their own time, and make sure they take time with other family or friends to help reassure them you all are still there.

Reinforce that connection, and don't allow that distance to grow. It may be difficult not to be upset. You have a right to be, which is recognized—but take your own frustration someplace else, into another room, or wait until they are not home. Don't let that frustration and anger fuel their thought process that the distance is okay and makes life easier.

There are things to watch for that can be harmful and need to be dealt with as quickly as possible. You may notice your loved one is drinking more heavily than usual. This is a sign there is more going on than they want you to know. There are first responders who know how to deal with their anxiety and depression in different ways, such as golf, fishing, hunting, or whatever they decide is their therapy. However, there are others who turn to alcohol, like I discussed earlier in the book—and an excessive amount of it.

Their consumption could become an even bigger issue personally and professionally, causing them to become angry quicker, furthering their depression, and leading to issues at work such as excessive force complaints, written reprimands, a suspension, or worse. It can be a difficult situation to be placed in, but don't be afraid to say something to the officer at this point.

Let them know you are aware they are drinking more than normal; they need to know they are changing and that it needs to be dealt with in a healthy way. But don't use it against them in the form of threats. At this point, they may not care, thinking it's just one more thing on their plate and a further reason to continue drinking or to start drinking more.

As I have mentioned before, suicide is a real threat among first responders and a major concern for everyone involved. Even though you don't want to push them to talk about their day or week, they do need to talk about what may be getting them to the point of self-harm. This may not happen with friends or family, but it needs to happen—even if with a professional.

They need to understand they are not alone and that there is help for them, even if it's through others in the field. There are several places where they can go, and many people they can talk to. You need to point them in the right direction. If this help doesn't come soon, it may be too late. Learn what signs to watch for, such as anxiety and depression. Work to convince them that seeking help is not a weakness and that it's available in so many places.

Remember, I'm only providing an understanding here of what first responders go through during their careers. It is not definite that all first responders will face the same challenges or have to deal with the same types of incidents. But this does give an idea of what many face, and I hope it gives an understanding of why some responders become angry, anxious, or distant. We may not be able to stop all suicides, but by keeping a keen eye on our first responders, my hope is that we can lower the rate and save the lives of many. We may even be able to lower the issues of excessive force by watching out for those we work with, noticing the changes in them and the increased anger, and maybe taking over as the primary officer on the scene so as not to allow an at-risk responder to go too far.

I hope the information in this book helps those wanting to get into law enforcement or other first-responder careers, along with those close to them, understand what first responders go through and have to deal with. Those who want to pursue such a career need to have an understanding of what to expect. You can go through all the schooling and training possible and think you know the effects these jobs can have. However, it's not until you actually start doing the work that you truly see the reality. Friends and family: Look out for those on tough jobs, like law enforcement. You have the ability to help make sure everyone makes it out in one piece, both physically and mentally.

If you or anyone you know is thinking about suicide, suffering from a mental health crisis, or suffering from addiction there is help for you. Below is a list of resources to use, remember, YOU ARE NOT ALONE, YOU MATTER!

Suicide Prevention Hotline
1-800-273-TALK (8255)

Crisis Text Line
Text BLUE to 741741

CopLine
1-800-COP-Line (1-800-267-5463)

POPPA
1-888-cops-cop (1-888-267-7267)

Blue Line Support
1-855-964-2583

Responder Strong
Text BADGE to 741-741
Or 206-459-3020

Frontline Helpline
1-866-676-7500

Fire/EMS Helpline
1-888-275-6832

Russell Ford spent 20 years in law enforcement before retiring. During his time on the road, he also served as a volunteer firefighter in a small mountain community. While in law enforcement he served ten years as a part-time SWAT officer and spent time filling many different positions on the team. He also has been a field training officer and specialized instructor in many disciplines. He is currently a college professor, teaching criminal justice and forensic psychology classes having a Ph.D. in Psychology with a focus on Forensic Psychology.

Made in the USA
Monee, IL
02 December 2024